Making Rights Claim

MAKING RIGHTS CLAIMS

A Practice of Democratic
Citizenship

KAREN ZIVI

OXFORD
UNIVERSITY PRESS

Oxford University Press, Inc., publishes works that further
Oxford University's objective of excellence
in research, scholarship, and education.

Oxford   New York
Auckland   Cape Town   Dar es Salaam   Hong Kong   Karachi
Kuala Lumpur   Madrid   Melbourne   Mexico City   Nairobi
New Delhi   Shanghai   Taipei   Toronto

With offices in
Argentina   Austria   Brazil   Chile   Czech Republic   France   Greece
Guatemala   Hungary   Italy   Japan   Poland   Portugal   Singapore
South Korea   Switzerland   Thailand   Turkey   Ukraine   Vietnam

Published by Oxford University Press, Inc.
198 Madison Avenue, New York, New York 10016

www.oup.com

Oxford is a registered trademark of Oxford University Press

Library of Congress Cataloging-in-Publication Data
Zivi, Karen.
Making rights claims: a practice of democratic citizenship /Karen Zivi.
    p.   cm.
Includes bibliographical references and index.
ISBN 978-0-19-982640-7 (pbk.: alk. paper)—ISBN 978-0-19-982641-4 (cloth: alk. paper)
1. Human rights. 2. Civil rights. I. Title.
JC571.Z58   2011
323—dc22   2011009251

1 3 5 7 9 8 6 4 2

Printed in the United States of America
on acid-free paper

To my mother and father, Sue and Lou Zivi. For all their patience and support.

Contents

Acknowledgments

TO WRITE A book is to make a claim in and upon the world. And like the claims to rights that I explore in the pages to come, it is an activity that is only made possible and given meaning by and through the relationships and networks in which we are embedded. I owe an enormous debt of gratitude to many people and institutions for making both possible and meaningful the activity of which these pages are but a small manifestation. They have been more generous with their time and resources than anyone has—dare I say—a *right* to expect.

This book began in the lively graduate seminars that made the Rutgers University program in political science such a special place to study political theory and women and politics. It was inspired and nurtured by a faculty and graduate student cohort that embraced and encouraged disparate approaches to the study of political thought, with an ongoing commitment to bringing theory to bear on political practice and a willingness to take questions of gender seriously. My deepest thanks go to the members of my dissertation committee who helped shepherd an early incarnation of this project. Linda Zerilli taught me to read widely and think broadly, to take intellectual risks and to be bold. She set a standard for excellence that I continue to aspire to today. Mary Hawkesworth brought a fresh perspective on and an enthusiasm for this project at precisely the time I needed it most, and she remains an exemplary scholar, teacher, and mentor. Gordon Schochet talked to me for hours about everything and anything, reminding me to see connections between ideas and practices where one might not usually look. And Timothy Kaufman-Osborn, though not a Rutgers professor, had such a profound impact on the make-up of the graduate student population there that I wanted my own piece of his legacy. I thank him for his guidance and his students.

The openness to varied ways of thinking about and doing political theory that was characteristic of the faculty at Rutgers attracted a group of students equally as engaging. I consider myself extremely fortunate, and will forever be thankful and proud, to be a part of a cohort that includes the likes of Farid Abdel-Nour, Cristina Beltran, Mark Brown, David Gutterman, Priti Joshi (a political theorist by another name), Jennet Kirkpatrick, Jill Locke, Laurie Naranch, Ronnee Schreiber, and Claire Snyder-Hall.

What began in New Jersey was nurtured and groomed, sometimes quite differently, in Massachusetts and California. In Harvard University's Social Studies program, I found one of the most stimulating intellectual homes a political theorist could ever ask for, and, in Katy Arnold, Verity Smith, and most especially Christina Tarnopolsky, amazing interlocutors and good friends. If my stay at Harvard deepened my understanding of the historical contours of social and political thought, my sojourn in the Department of Political Science at the University of Southern California brought me back to questions of identity in contemporary politics. Janelle Wong and Ricardo Ramirez were especially important in making me feel a part of the Trojan family. I then finished the manuscript while at the University of Richmond's Jepson School of Leadership Studies. Many colleagues at Jepson and the University as a whole have been generous with their feedback and support, but particular thanks go to Liz Faier, Crystal Hoyt, Ana Mitric, and Thad Williamson, for endless conversations about the meaning of leadership and justice and for the accompanying comic relief and hard ciders.

No academic book comes to fruition without having been vetted in various ways at conferences and in workshops. For their questions, advice, and provocations, I thank the organizers and participants of the Western Political Science Association's Feminist Theory Workshop; USC's Center for Law, History, and Culture; UCLA's Center for the Study of Women and the Political Theory Workshop; the University of Virginia's Political Theory Colloquium; Drexel University's Great Works Symposium; and Johns Hopkins University's Women, Gender, and Sexuality Program Workshop. This project would not have been possible without generous financial support from the Rutgers University Department of Political Science, the Social Science Research Council, and the Bonner Center for Civic Engagement at the University of Richmond. Portions of chapter 3 previously appeared as "Cultivating Character: John Stuart Mill and the Subject of Rights," *American Journal of Political Science*, 50, no.1 (2006); portions of chapter 4 as "Feminism and the Politics of Rights: A Qualified Defense of Identity-Based Rights Claiming," *Politics & Gender*, 1, no. 3 (2005), and portions of chapter 5 as "Contesting Motherhood in the Age of AIDS: Maternal Ideology in the Debate over Mandatory HIV Testing," *Feminist Studies* 31, no. 2 (2005). I thank these journals for allowing me to reprint this material.

I also want to thank the countless members of the academic community who have inspired, encouraged, and engaged me and this work over the years. In particular, Paul Apostolidis, Benjamin Barber, Rick Battistoni, Lawrie Balfour, Jane Bennett, Bill Connolly, Shannon Connolly, Jodi Dean, Joshua Foa Diestag, Lisa Disch, Nancy Hirschmann, Bonnie Honig, Kirstie McClure, Jeanne Morefield, Paul Passavant, Davide Panagia, Andrew Rehfeld, Austin Sarat, Torrey Shanks, and Zoe Silverman have shaped this manuscript in ways both subtle and profound. So, too, have the "anonymous" readers who reviewed my work at crucial stages in the process. We should all be so lucky to be on the receiving end of feedback from the likes of Terrell Carver, Sam Chambers, Don Herzog, Patchen Markell, Lori Marso, and Liz Wingrove. Their generosity and perspicacity astound me still.

An extraordinary group of friends, both old and new, provided the deep well of support, advice, and humor I needed to finish the book. My writing buddies, Michaele Ferguson, Jill Locke, Lori Marso, and Holloway Sparks, were always there with constructive criticism, good cheer, and the kind of amusing anecdotes that keep one grounded. Though they are all my "balcony people," Michaele was this project's true champion. She read more drafts of the manuscript than anyone else, and it is far better because of her acuity and encouragement. Though I should probably keep this secret to myself, there really is no better way to challenge and sharpen one's arguments than to share them with Michaele. I also want to acknowledge the dear friends who are part of my extended family around the country. Joanne Fernando, Suzanne Strulowitz, Liz Braunstein, Blair Smith, Jennifer and Isabella Pearson, Ana Mitric, Ronnee Schreiber, and Laurie Naranch have known me at my best and my worst and, nonetheless, continue to provide care, respite, and perspective when wanted and needed. These women are the sisters we should all have. And a special thanks go to Janelle Wong, David Silver, Evan Song, and Rexx for sharing their home, their laughter, their food, their clothing, their car, and their love with me during the fall of 2010.

And, of course, my family. My mother and father-in-law, Jean and Phil Nelson, opened their hearts and home to me, shared their family and friends with me, and continue to help me make a home wherever I am, and for that I will always be grateful. Mark Moody, Leann Yoder, Logan and Adrienne Moody, and Margie and Harvey Willensky were always willing to provide reasons to have some fun and never tired, thank goodness, of encouraging me to loosen up. I thank my brother, Jeff Zivi, for all the sage professional, personal, and TV-related advice he has offered over the years, for reminding me that not everyone thinks as I do, and for digging the ditches and painting the walls that made my first house a home. And to my parents, Sue and Louis Zivi, where do I even begin? Thank you to my mother for sharing her love of books and big ideas with me, for encouraging intellectual curiosity, and for daring to be different. I thank my father for the unconditional love and commitment to family and home that sustains me on a daily basis, particularly when supplemented by dozens of bagels.

Last, but certainly not least, I want to thank Michael Moody. He has been my best friend and intellectual raconteur for almost two decades. He makes me laugh, gives me space to cry, and helps me stretch and grow in ways that I cannot always imagine. He saw a book where I could only see a pile of papers, and he envisions a bright future when I get stuck in the past. He is also a model, for me, of what it means to be engaged in the world of ideas and of people. I will always remember him as the guy who put plastic bags on his dress shoes in order to push a stranger's car from a snow bank during the blizzard of 1993. Michael offered me a glimpse into who he is and what it means to give back that day, and he continues to surprise and delight me.

Making Rights Claims

1

From Rights to Rights Claiming

A CHINESE DISSIDENT committed to bringing democracy to his country claims that the rights to speak and associate freely are human rights that his government must respect, and for this he is put in jail. A conservative church group goes before the U.S. Supreme Court to defend their First Amendment right to denounce homosexuality at the funerals of military personnel, and though condemned by much of the political left, they are joined in their rights claiming by the American Civil Liberties Union and the *New York Times*. A group of women in Iran make claims for women's rights as human rights and, in so doing, put their lives and their commitment to their own culture on the line. AIDS activists in South Africa take their young democratic government to court to demand that it live up to its promise to protect and promote the health-care rights of its citizens, and consequently they stand accused of getting into bed with the capitalist interests of multinational pharmaceutical companies. Muslims in France test the limits of democratic toleration by demanding the right to wear head scarves in public schools, but they lose. Gays and lesbians in the United States take their fight for marriage rights to court despite being condemned by conservatives for undermining the democratic process and by members of their own constituency for betraying a commitment to sexual diversity. Feminists the world over continue to make claims for women's right to reproductive freedom even though they face charges of perpetuating a callous individualism that threatens the fabric of community.

As these examples suggest, we make rights claims for a wide variety of reasons: to call for an end to physical abuse and political oppression, to demand a response to public health crises, to chastise governments for inaction in the face of natural disasters, to insist on global engagement in times of genocide or famine, to question or defend military intervention in other nations, and to shore up or tear down the walls that make portions of our lives "private." We make rights claims to criticize practices we find objectionable, to shed light on injustice, to limit the power of government, and to demand state accountability and intervention. Indeed, if the 1960s marked a "rights revolution" in the United States, one might say that the late twentieth and early twenty-first centuries have been witness to this revolution's spread around the globe.[1] People the world over are calling for the enforcement of various political and civil rights identified in the United Nations Universal Declaration of Human Rights (UNDHR), demanding the extension of these rights to new groups or situations, and even making claims for heretofore unnamed social, economic, and cultural rights—such as the right to health care and sexuality.[2] At the same time, international governing bodies are writing and rewriting rights declarations and covenants, creating new committees and institutions to monitor and protect these rights, and working with local communities to turn general rights norms into specific public policy. Though not everyone agrees on when this modern age of rights began or what precisely spurred it, there is little debate that rights language has become a dominant discourse of politics and the public good, rights claiming a practice of everyday life.[3]

That we now live in what could be described as an era or a culture of rights is not surprising given that rights claiming has a palpable moral and political appeal. Claims for rights of all sorts are closely associated with valued principles such as equality and human freedom, as well as precious victories in the struggle to end practices of oppression or to advance a more just society.[4] Rights claiming is celebrated for instilling a sense of pride in our past and inspiring hope for future change, for having what Patricia Williams describes as the "alchemical" capacity to make us feel powerful and purposeful, often transforming us from disenfranchised individuals into engaged political actors.[5] In recent years, rights claiming has even been championed for bringing people together by offering a vision of justice that resonates across borders, ethnicities, and religions. At the same time, as the above examples also suggest, rights claiming has been and continues to be a suspect and risky practice of political engagement, particularly for those committed to advancing something called democracy. People who have come of age with or in the wake of the civil rights revolution, the women's movement, the struggle for gay rights, and the proliferation of global human rights campaigns might think it odd to question the relationship between democracy and rights—as Jeremy Waldron explains, the very word *democracy* has become a shorthand for human rights.[6] But the relationship between rights and democracy is not, and has never been, so clear-cut. As historians remind us, democracy and rights have quite distinct conceptual and political genealogies that are themselves the subject of significant debate: while most scholars agree that democracy had its birth in ancient Greece, there is little consensus on whether rights, or the idea of rights, can be found in ancient times and across various cultures, or only comes into being during the European and American revolutions of the eighteenth century, the crafting of the UNDHR, or even more recently.[7] Perhaps even more important, there is little agreement about whether rights claiming is a valuable democratic practice. This is due, to a some extent, to the fact that democracy itself is a contested concept. While some use the term to capture a particular institutional configuration or practice of self-governance defined as the rule of the people or the will of the majority, others use the term to refer to a particular political value or priority such as freedom, equality, or civic engagement. And even when there is some agreement about what democracy means, there is often debate about whether or not rights are an effective means of enacting, sustaining, or engendering it. Rights claims, or at least rights claims of a certain kind, are often meant to limit the power of the people themselves, and rights claims are not always efficacious. We certainly know from the history of rights politics that whether rights are claimed in courtrooms or on the streets, in the United States or beyond, by individuals or groups, or by conservatives or progressives, winning a right, let alone claiming it, has never guaranteed its protection or its exercise or brought the promises of democratic freedom to fruition.[8] That rights claiming has been unable to eradicate or even fully constrain the violence, tyranny, dire living conditions, and injustices that make life unbearable for some has been and continues to be extraordinarily frustrating. When rights campaigns fail to bring an end to political debate and controversy, when they result in a change in the law but not in practice, when they are simply ignored, or when they produce results that are at odds with our expectations, we end up disappointed, surprised, and even angry, and we often seek out alternative strategies of political contestation or work to fix what appears to be a broken system.

Contemporary political theorists who study rights have a variety of explanations for and responses to these challenges. Among democratic theorists, even those who disagree philosophically or politically, there is a sense that the problems with rights go far beyond their legal or political failures and have roots deep in their philosophical premises. Communitarians, critical legal scholars, feminists, critical race theorists, and others question the ability of rights (e.g., rights-based political activities, rights-based moral justifications, rights-based legal efforts) to promote democratic change and they call attention to rights' tendency to reinforce everything from atomistic individualism and Western imperialism to capitalist exploitation and patriarchal masculinity.[9] They point out that rights claiming can make us antagonistic toward others and blind to our complicity in practices of domination; and that it can, and likely will, have a chilling effect on the democratic decision making, participatory politics, and creative contestation that make democracy so appealing. For some of these scholars, the negative effects of rights claiming are so deeply tied to the way rights have been conceptualized historically and practiced politically that it is best if we simply leave rights behind and seek out a new language or style of political contestation.[10] For others, of course, continuing the "rights revolution" remains a valuable pursuit; under the proper conditions, rights-based efforts can and will advance democratic values and practice. Yet even these scholars who are more optimistic about the potential of rights disagree about what it will take to make rights work—or work better—to advance democracy. Some suggest that the solution to the problem of rights lies in articulating a more comprehensive philosophical foundation of rights, while other suggest that conceptual clarification of the term is necessary. Still others suggest that we need to craft a more inclusive set of rights or create institutions and procedures that are better able to protect and ensure rights.

If rights critics are correct, those engaged in a politics of rights claiming are committing serious philosophical and political errors. Not only are they failing to realize that rights are conceptually problematic, perhaps even "nonsense upon stilts," as Jeremy Bentham once suggested, but they are also allowing rights-based political efforts to undermine the democratic advances they seek to make. If, on the other hand, rights advocates are correct, then it is the critics who have made a mistake, overestimating the negative effects of rights claiming or underestimating the compromises that the practical realities of politics necessitate. There could, of course, be a third option. Perhaps we are now living in a new era of rights, an age in which the problems that once concerned rights critics—such as their political ineffectiveness or their tendency to be counter-majoritarian, culturally imperialistic, or economically exploitative, perhaps even their complicity in perpetuating democratically debilitating forms of self-interest or male privilege—have been overcome through new ways of theorizing, institutionalizing, or practicing rights. Maybe we now have the correct conception or comprehensive list of rights, or perhaps even the foolproof procedure for making rights claims, that will get us beyond the concerns about their prior incompatibility with democratic aspirations, values, and practices.[11]

So, how are we to make sense of the fact that rights claiming is simultaneously ubiquitous and disparaged, embraced and decried? Such radically different perspectives on the meaning of rights and the relationship between rights and democracy can leave scholars—not to mention lawyers, activists, and the general public—with their heads spinning. It certainly leaves those interested in the project of democracy, however imagined, with some difficult questions to address. Should individuals and groups seeking democratic justice and equality use the language of rights to advance their goals? If so, how and why? Which rights should be claimed, under what conditions, and for what purposes? How can they be secured and what exactly do they secure? And if not rights, why not? What alternative might better advance democracy? In this book, I suggest that such questions may be premature. It is not that rights' champions have embraced a naïve belief in their emancipatory potential or that skeptics are too far removed from the realities of political life to recognize their value. Nor is it the case that we now live in a rights era in which the problematic relationship between rights and democracy has been reconciled. Such explanations for, as well as condemnations of, the increasing popularity of rights claiming around the world are too simplistic, for the relationship between rights and democracy is less a problem to be solved than it is a relationship to be understood anew.

Making Rights Claims seeks to understand what it is about rights that make them at once an increasingly popular global language of political reform and a continued target of philosophical and political critique. As I suggest in the pages that follow, the answer lies in understanding their *democratic character*. That is, rights language remains of value for political movements committed to advancing democratic values and practices because it is through the making of rights claims that we contest and constitute the meaning of individual identity, the contours of community, and the forms that political subjectivity take. Rights claiming is a practice that allows us to question and reconstitute the very meaning of what is common or sensible and what is not, and this is, as some democratic theorists remind us, precisely what it means to engage in democratic politics.[12] Nonetheless, doing this work of questioning, contesting, and

revising, of learning about and practicing the art of democratic citizenship in whatever form it takes, is no panacea for the ills and injustices
that we confront. We must understand, then, that rights claiming is a
democratic practice because it opens up rather than shuts down the possibility for political engagement and thus demands our ongoing political
participation—something we may or may not fully welcome.

From Rights to Rights Claiming

To shed light on what I am calling the democratic character of rights and
rights claiming, I suggest that we first need to acquire some new conceptual tools or a fresh perspective on and approach to understanding what
rights are and what they do. For this, I draw on resources from the philosophy of language and, in particular, those contemporary strands of speech
act theory that look closely at notions of performativity.[13] It is my contention that to recognize the democratic character of rights we must understand rights claims as *performative utterances* and rights claiming as a
performative practice. Though in the coming pages I say more about what
it means to take a performative perspective on rights, let me point out here
that at its most basic level, a theory of performativity reminds us that
speaking or communicating in any way is an activity that does far more
than simply describe an already existing reality or make sounds. It reminds
us that our speaking is a social practice: our utterances entail a variety of
activities that occur between and among people who are themselves situated in the context of social norms and customs. This means that speaking
is a practice through which we both represent *and* shape, reflect *and* constitute the world in which we live. Our utterances are, in other words,
often simultaneously statements of fact and generative activities that
involve speakers and listeners in a process of citing, interpreting, and even
reshaping background norms, rules, and conventions. To approach rights
and rights claiming from the perspective of performativity means, then,
asking questions not simply about what a right *is* but also about what it is
we *do* when we make rights claims. It means attending to the ways in
which the making of a claim such as "I have a right to *X*" does far more
than accurately (or perhaps inaccurately) represent a pre-existing moral,
legal, or political reality. And it means appreciating that a seemingly
simple utterance such as "The people have a right to self-governance" is
always far more than a single sentence; it is, instead, a complex activity

more akin, perhaps, to telling a story or crafting a particular perspective on the present and the future.

Unlike scholars who approach rights as some kind of empirically veri-fiable fact about the world, or who depict rights claiming as the singular practice of constraining or trumping, I approach rights claiming as an activity or, rather, set of activities through which we shape—indeed, at times constitute—our world and our selves.[14] This is not to suggest that rights have no existence as legal facts or moral principles. It is, instead, to shift or expand the way we study both the philosophy and the practice of rights. A performative perspective on rights moves us from an almost exclusive focus on questions about what rights *are* to a more careful con-sideration of what it is rights *do;* from a tendency to treat rights as things or instruments we use to bring about a particular end to a recognition that rights claiming is a complex linguistic activity, the outcomes of which are quite often beyond our complete control. A performative perspective on rights, in other words, moves us beyond concerns about the formal defini-tions of rights and allows us to take seriously rights claiming as a social and political practice.[15]

Making Rights Claims is a book that sheds light not only on what is democratic about the practice of rights claiming but also on how it is that we come to see that. It thus brings philosophical approaches to the study of rights together with sociological and anthropological ones and concerns itself with how dominant approaches to the study of rights theory may constrain our understanding of both rights theory and rights practice. The emphasis of the book is dual: I engage in a performative analysis of both how we think about or theorize rights and what we do in our everyday practice of making rights claims. This approach may frustrate some, par-ticularly those who are eager to determine what philosophical, legal, or institutional bases have or will effectively ensure specific political or social change, or what precisely is happening in a particular rights campaign. These are common and understandable desires expressed by activists and scholars alike. Certainly one of the fundamental reasons for making rights claims is to put an end to injustice, misery, violence, and other harms once and for all—and we want to know exactly what worked or went wrong in a particular instance so as to learn from the past and ensure a particular future. However, the impulse to seek philosophical justifications, laws, or political institutions that will put an end to such problems, or to offer the definitive reading of a particular political practice, assumes an under-standing of the role of political theory or conceptual analysis—as well as the meaning of both democratic politics and rights—that I want to question. Here, then, I follow Isaiah Berlin, who suggests that the project of political theory is not to offer a blueprint for effective action or to provide irrefutable philosophical justifications for particular claims; it is, instead, "an inquiry concerned . . . with the critical examination of presuppositions and assumptions, and the question of the order of priorities and ultimate ends . . . [in] a society in which there is not total acceptance of any single end."[16] Political theory, on this account, is part of an effort to make visible dominant ways of thinking so that we can recognize their value and their limits, so they can be modified or rejected if need be, always knowing full well that the modifications suggested are open to contestation. *Making Rights Claims* is, at its heart, a political theoretical investigation of rights.

This is, however, a political theoretical investigation that recognizes the importance of taking theory and practice as objects of study. In other words, I examine both philosophical arguments and political practices from a performative perspective. I use insights drawn from various strands of speech act theory to expose a dominant way of thinking that has important implications for our ability to assess—indeed, understand—the democratic character of rights practice and I then explore contemporary rights practice for its performative qualities and characteristics. I begin with an analysis of rights theory because, as I detail in the pages that follow, there is a tendency—common to both academic and everyday understandings of rights—to treat rights as objects or things that we have, the way we have arms or legs, and that we put to use for various purposes. This way of thinking about rights appears in work that is critical as well as optimistic about the democratic potential of rights; that represents liberal, communitarian, and poststructuralist perspectives on rights; and that defends rights as particular claims, as well as that which defends rights as universals. This incredibly varied scholarship, in addition to conceiving of rights as objects or artifacts, tends to reduce rights claims to statements about the world that can be verified or falsified or to depict them as purely instrumental claims whose democratic effect and outcome we can or should be able to control. As I argue, this dominant way of understanding, and thus of analyzing, rights and rights claiming fails to appreciate the full array of generative activities that occur when we make rights claims and, in particular, gives scant attention to the important intersubjective and contextually located dimensions of the practice. This in turn clouds our ability to see what is promising and problematic, valuable and dangerous about contemporary rights-based political activities.

But what, then, do I mean by a *right* and which *rights* am I talking about: legal or moral; individual or human rights; civil, political, cultural, or economic rights; equal or special rights; the rights of individuals, groups, corporations, women, children, or immigrants? Such are the questions I am asked again and again whenever I say I am writing a book about rights. My answer is a somewhat paradoxical one: I am writing about all of these kinds of rights and yet none of them. On the one hand, I am interested in what is happening in and through the process of making a rights claim, irrespective of the specific kind of rights claim being made, and I suggest that a performative analysis can and should be applied to almost any kind of rights theorizing or rights politics. On the other hand, because a performative analysis draws our attention to the interpersonal and sociolinguistic context in which a specific claim is made, it reminds us that different claims reference different conventions and resonate in varied ways. Making a claim for a right to privacy is not the same as making a claim for a right to health care, and making a claim for a right to health care may be heard by different people in fundamentally different ways. Indeed, as T. H. Marshall has so aptly illustrated, it is often the case that particular kinds of rights come into being at distinct moments in time, engaging vastly different institutions, imagining the relationship between individuals in opposing manners, and finding justification in antithetical philosophical or religious traditions.[17] But even a claim to a very specific economic, social, or political right, as speech act theory reminds us, is never a singular utterance or act; it is, instead, a set of activities that should be analyzed for the varied effects it has have on the world. In other words, a performative analysis recognizes the value in identifying and distinguishing between and among not just different kinds of rights claims but also the different acts and effects that may be entailed in a single claim.

I thus locate the practice of making rights claims in something we might describe as a larger *rights culture*. While others refer to this phenomenon as "rights talk" or "rights discourse," I call it a culture, in the constructivist sense of the word, to emphasize that the thing we call "rights" is actually a dynamic set of ideas, norms, and practices, rather than a static philosophical concept or a singular political practice. To think of rights as a culture, in other words, means appreciating that it is an ever-changing conglomeration of stories, rituals, beliefs, and practices. It means recognizing that it is a linguistic construct that is both captured in and produced by language users who continually reshape it through the stories they tell about whom they are and how they relate to each other. Rights culture therefore must be treated as an object, or a series of objects (stories, rituals, traditions, etc.) that can be identified and studied, *and* an activity, or something we do with others to create our sense of self and community.[18] The emphasis on the constructed nature of culture reminds us, then, to contextualize the practice of rights claiming, to see it as contributing to the often shared but contested stories that form the conceptual apparatus or background of what we know about and do with rights. For example, *rights culture* includes the belief that rights represent or symbolize those especially important goods that make human flourishing possible; it contains the idea that individual rights entail corresponding duties or obligations on the part of other individuals, groups, or institutions; and it provides a series of reasons or stories for these intuitions. Rights culture also includes understandings of what it means to make rights claims: if we believe that rights represent goods of such great importance that they should take priority over other political and social considerations, then we come to expect that when we make a rights claim we are offering such a powerful argument for addressing an injustice or making a change that it warrants constraining the actions and behavior of other individuals and institutions.[19] Though our rights claims may not always succeed at this kind of "trumping," we certainly hope and expect that they will. The set of intuitions and practices that make up rights culture include, then, a common sensibility that rights are special objects or instruments that help define the relationships between and among individuals, communities, institutions, and states. Indeed, it is often this cultural background that allows us to understand what a person means and is trying to do when she makes a rights claim in the courtroom or on the streets, whether or not that rights claim is coincident with positive law or exercisable or enforceable in the immediate or foreseeable future.[20]

Of course, I do not mean to suggest that rights culture is monolithic. It should be understood as consisting of a variety of stories, not all of which are consistent and many of which are open to multiple and conflicting interpretations. For example, while there may be a dominant narrative about rights as individualistic trumps that are the birthright of human beings, there are competing narratives about rights as constructed by societies. Differing accounts exist of what actually counts as a right (e.g., health care, cultural traditions, sexual expression) and about who has rights (e.g., an individual, a community, a fetus, a tree, an animal, women), as well as about what and who is required to protect and promote such rights. Take the example of claiming a right to clean air or a right to health care. We may understand, on a general level, both what these claims mean and what the claimant is trying to do through making the claim, and yet we may not all agree that clean air or health care is legitimately or best characterized as a "right." Even if we agree that these goods are aptly called rights, we may disagree about what promoting and protecting such rights entails on the part of individuals, communities, and governments. We may value clean air but not more than we value the freedom to smoke or to access inexpensive energy. We might also value access to good health care but not consider it the responsibility of the government to provide financial resources to make access a reality, particularly if such government expenditures threaten social order or national security. Of course, even when we agree that something is a right and that it should be a priority and lead to change, we may have quite different interpretations of what that change should look like. We might agree that health care is an important good, even a human right, but disagree about how extensive it should be or about from where funds should come to provide it. And yet, despite such disagreements and diversity of perspectives, there remains a degree of comprehensibility about the meaning of these rights claims: we can still understand, at least on some level, what someone means when he or she uses the term "right." When we understand rights as an ever-changing culture rather than a clearly bounded concept then we can appreciate that debates about what rights are or how best to ensure them are not indicative, necessarily, of conceptual flaws or a political missteps, but are, rather, constitutive of rights themselves. What is important, then, is to become aware of how these ideas and practices shape individual and group identity, and how they are transformed by people, groups, and institutions.

As a result of this orientation to rights, *Making Rights Claims* does not fit neatly into the traditional types of philosophical analyses of rights; it does not provide a formal definition of a right, offer a typology of different rights claims, or take a stand in the debates between will and interest theorists of rights or liberal defenders and their communitarian critics.[21] Nor does the book take a firm stand on whether rights are timeless and universal norms or historically specific effects of particular configurations of power.[22] Though I lean toward an understanding of rights claims as socially and politically constructed concepts—discursive objects the meaning and power of which change over time—my purpose in this book is neither to take a position on these competing conceptions of rights nor to reconcile them. Instead, I follow Joel Feinberg's suggestion, made more than thirty years ago, that attempts at a formal definition or theory of rights often leads us in circles and, thus, if we seek to understand the value of rights, particularly for the practice of democracy, it is important to study the kind of activity that rights claiming entails.[23] This, then, is why the focus of the book is on the *making* of rights claims.

Performative Utterances

Treating rights claims as performative utterances and rights claiming as a performative practice means paying attention to what happens in and through the making of such claims. To do that, I suggest we draw on insights from speech act theory, particularly those contemporary iterations that may be more familiar as theories of performativity. I argue, in other words, that rights claiming should be understood as a performative practice and that this performativity is what makes the practice an essential component of a robust democratic politics. But what exactly is a performative practice and how does a performative perspective reveal the democratic character of rights and rights claiming? Answering the second part of that question is the task of the book as a whole. Here, let me say a few words about a performative perspective itself. While the concept of performativity is likely familiar to some readers, particularly those who are interested in gender and sexuality studies, it is often the case that we mean different things by the same term. I offer the following overview of my understanding of performativity in an effort to dispel possible misconceptions or confusions among those familiar with the concept, as well as to introduce key terms to those for whom it may be new.

In making a case for investigating and understanding rights claims as performative utterances, I draw on the speech act theory of J. L. Austin and the writings of some of his contemporary interlocutors such as Jacques Derrida, Stanley Cavell, and Judith Butler. This body of scholarship emphasizes the ways in which speaking, as well as writing and other forms of communication, produces rather than simply reflects our world. At the heart of this understanding of linguistic activity is the Austinian distinction between constative and performative utterances, between those speech acts that can be verified empirically, because they state facts about the world, and those that cannot and yet remain comprehensible. Utterances such as "the cat is on the mat" and "I am holding a shoe" are examples of constative utterances that describe the world in which we live and thus can be assessed as true or false. We can look to see if, in fact, the *cat* is on the mat or if the cat is on the *mat*, if I am *holding* a shoe or I am holding a *shoe*. But there are many other utterances that are understandable despite their being empirically unverifiable. Austin designates this class of utterances as performatives because of their world-making capacity: because of the fact that it is in the saying that the act is done. His classic examples of performative utterances include "I do," "I bet," and "I name thee"—utterances that neither "describe my doing of what I should be said in so uttering to be doing [n]or state that I am doing it."[24] In making the utterance, we actually do the very thing of which we speak. For example, in the process of saying "I name thee," the speaker engages in the act of naming rather than describing what she did in the past or will do in the future. "I name thee" is thus not a representation of an already existing reality—it cannot be verified as true or false—and yet it is a comprehensible utterance.[25]

Such oft-cited examples of performative utterances do not, however, tell us everything about what a performative is or does. Indeed, "I bet" and "I do" belong to a category of explicit performatives that Austin eventually sets aside. As he comes to realize in the course of his thinking about speech activity, the constative/performative distinction does not actually hold for *all* utterances. Even those utterances that seem to be explicitly descriptive have performative dimensions. Take the statement "There is a bee near your head," for example. Certainly we can check to see if the statement matches some reality and there is indeed a bee somewhere near your head. But the utterance has a force and effects that are not captured by this understanding. A speaker may be saying "There is a bee near your head" as a shortcut to warning you about the bee, and the utterance may alarm you because you are allergic. Or a speaker may say it to warn you because she is allergic, but you may react with joy because you are, unbeknownst to the speaker, an enthusiastic bee keeper who has been looking for a bee all day. What is important here, then, is not whether the utterance is constative or performative exclusively; what is important is the kind of performance or performances the utterance entails. For this, we need Austin's tripartite distinction captured in what he calls the "total speech situation." The total speech situation entails three acts: the locutionary, the illocutionary, and the perlocutionary. The locutionary act refers to what is said or the sounds one makes, the illocutionary act refers to what one does *in* saying something, and the perlocutionary act refers to what one does *by* saying something. If a speaker says "I bet" in the course of a card game, for example, she is making a series of noises (locution), engaging in the act of betting (illocution), and having an effect on the subjective states of her fellow players and other listeners (perlocution).

I am suggesting that we treat claims such as "I have a right to privacy" or "We have a right to health care" as performative utterances, asking not just whether the particular claim corresponds to law or morality as if it were simply a constative utterance but also what it is a speaker *does* in and by making a particular claim. We need to analyze rights claiming, in other words, as an illocutionary and a perlocutionary activity. Attending to this distinction is important for a number of reasons: it draws our attention to the context in which a claim is made, it demands that we pay serious attention to the role that social norms and conventions play in turning our noise making into comprehensible utterances, and it reminds us that speaking is an intersubjective practice, an activity that occurs between and among speaking beings. It helps us to recognize that if a speaker in Massachusetts says "I have a right to marry someone of the same sex," he may be simply stating a fact, describing a legal and political reality embraced by the state. If, however, he were to make that claim in Ohio or Virginia, the speaker would be doing something quite different. To be sure, he could be simply making a statement that is legally false for certain and morally true only from some perspectives. On these accounts, we would say that the speaker is making a statement that can be verified or falsified empirically, and thus making a constative utterance. But to treat his utterance, or any rights claim for that matter, solely in terms of its empirical verifiability would, of course, be to miss the fact that the speaker's utterance performs a variety of activities. Indeed, it may be the case that when he makes the claim in Virginia, he is criticizing the decisions of the government and the people of the state. Or perhaps he is rallying supporters at a march or warning opponents of a coming legal battle. It may also be the case that the speaker's utterance has the effect of making listeners angry, excited, ashamed, or motivated to act. These accounts acknowledge the fact that we are always doing something both *in* and *by* making a rights claim, that a rights claim is not only a statement of fact or a locutionary act but also an illocutionary and a perlocutionary act.[26]

How exactly an utterance works to change or constitute the world around us is a matter of considerable debate. One of the most compelling explanations draws our attention to the *context* of the utterance—those social norms and conventions that a speaker references in the act of making noise. From this perspective, the fact that we do something in speaking has less to do with the specific words we use or even what we intend to do with the words we use and more to do with the social norms we reference when we speak.[27] This is particularly true with respect to the illocutionary dimensions of a speech act. As Pierre Bourdieu explains, words do not "possess *in themselves* the source of power"; rather, power "resides in the institutional conditions of their production and reception."[28] For example, a speaker may say "I do" to her best friend, but that does not mean she has married her unless, of course, she has done so in a certain context, in the presence of a certain set of officials, and in one of the few states that currently allows members of the same sex to marry. The speaker must meet a certain set of conditions or cite certain conventions in order to have gotten married in the process of saying "I do": if she says "I do" during the performance of play rather than in front of a properly designated official, these effects will not follow. The effectiveness or success of the utterance—what Austin often refers to as its *felicity* or *uptake*—is a matter of citing the proper conventions. Bourdieu describes this process as referencing "the combination of a systematic set of interdependent conditions which constitute social rituals,"[29] while Judith Butler describes it less as a discrete or intentional event and more as the result or "sedimentation" of conventions repeated on a regular basis.[30]

But even attention to the conditions that are referenced in speaking does not capture all of what it means for an utterance to be performative. Indeed, the performativity of an utterance often far exceeds reference to the conventions and conditions, the social norms and rules that speakers and listeners acknowledge or assume. As Austin suggests, the *perlocutionary* force of an utterance—what I do *by* saying something—is not determined by the conventions cited by the utterance. Perlocutionary effects are those that are actually decidedly unconventional. To illustrate the difference between conventional and unconventional effects of a speech act, take the example of the wedding ceremony again. If I say "I do" under the proper conditions (e.g., in front of a person vested with the authority to legalize a marriage to a member of a particular sex when we are both over a particular age, in front of an eyewitness), it will certainly lead to a change in my legal status and my relationship to another person. It may entitle me to new rights and generate new legal responsibilities. It may change my identity, both from my own and from others' perspectives. These are some of the illocutionary effects of the act. But my "I do" may also make some people very happy (my parents, for example) and others quite sad (a dear friend who misses a spouse lost at an unexpectedly early age), irrespective of whether social norms are being properly followed. That the utterance has an impact on the subjective state, of the listeners is neither dependent on nor dictated by social conventions. How people react to my saying "I do" may have nothing to do with the conditions under which I make the utterance or with the intention behind my saying it. These are the perlocutionary effects of my speech act. Or, take the example of betting: When I say "I bet six," I am clearly doing the thing I speak of; and, if I make the utterance during a game of poker or under other conditions in which betting makes sense, then I have engaged in a successful illocutionary act. The utterance might upset some listeners (I bet too much or too little) and make my competitors giddy, inspiring rather than shaking their confidence. These perlocutionary effects of the utterance have nothing to do with the conventions associated with betting, and they are effects over which I, as the speaker, have no control.

These examples suggest that speakers do not have perfect control over the outcomes of their utterances. They may cite the proper conventions, and make an utterance under all the proper conditions, and yet be surprised by the outcome or effects of their speech. Control over the felicity or success of an utterance is complicated by the fact that we are, as language users, individuals who come to be through language, and that language is itself both the site and the effect of social or intersubjective relationships. We do things *through*—rather than simply *with*—language. Speaking is an activity we do in relation to others, in the context of an already existing community; it is not only the convention itself that is a product of language—as subjects, we are as well. Put differently, we are, as Charles Taylor suggests, beings embedded in language whose utterances always occur within and are made intelligible by "a background which we can never fully dominate." At the same time, however, this is "a background that we are never fully dominated by." We may be unable to control this background completely, but we are not its simple dupes. Our relationship within and to language, the activity of making claims, is, then, a bit precarious: "we never fully know what we are doing to it; we develop language without knowing fully what we are making it into."[31] This means that the citing of conventions is itself a complicated and uncertain process. Even if an utterance cites all the conventions it is supposed to, and even if the correct words are used and the speaker's intention is clear, utterances can fail or go awry: words can be used out of context and can be misunderstood. This is the result of the fact that conventions themselves are linguistic constructs, norms that form the background in which we are embedded as individuals. These conventions, the rules of our language games, are themselves constituted through language and form our shared way of living; they are not simply ideas or norms that exist separate from people.[32] The citation of a convention—repeating certain words under the proper conditions in front of an authorized individual—is, then, never a perfect repetition of some clearly identifiable or locatable original rule. As Butler puts it, the force of a speech act is the effect of "a ritual chain of resignifications whose origin and end remain unfixed and unfixable."[33] Though the correct referencing of conventions may be part of what renders a performative utterance effective, it in no way guarantees that such outcomes will occur. This is due, in part, to the fact that the felicity of a claim is not assured simply by choosing the correct word for the situation, by having a specific intention, or by citing particular social norms. Indeed, given that speech acts occur in a social context and are, themselves, practices that occur between and among individuals, infelicities such as misinterpretations and misunderstandings are to be expected, even embraced.

Analyzing rights theory and practice from a performative perspective means, then, appreciating the extent to which our claims both reference and reiterate social conventions and norms, and yet have forces and effects that exceed them. The fact is that we always make rights claims in a complicated social context to others who may or may not recognize or understand a claim in precisely the way we expect. This contingency does not make rights claiming any less of an important practice to consider with respect to its democratic implications. Indeed, as I argue in the following pages, it is often because rights claiming cannot be perfectly captured in terms of a set of conventions and rules that it is valuable for democracy. To put the point differently, from the perspective of performativity, rights claiming is both a rule-bound and a rule-breaking practice that opens up the possibility of the new, and this is precisely what makes it suitable for contemporary democratic politics.

A theory of performativity thus offers a unique lens of analysis through which to examine the relationship between rights and democracy. It provides us with a set of categories and questions that push us beyond concerns with the philosophical or legal meaning of a rights claim and draws our attention to the effects or force of the activity of making such claims. A performative approach to understanding and studying rights means asking questions about what we are doing together when we say we have rights, about the realities we create and the relationships we engender through the making of rights claims, and about the effects that our utterances may have, intended or otherwise, on both ourselves and others. It reminds us that there is always a degree of uncertainty and unpredictability to this practice because the force or effect of our claims are influenced by, and in turn influence, the context—the sets of institutions, relationships, norms, and conventions—in which we and the multiple interlocutors to whom we speak are embedded. This makes rights claiming a central part of a robust democratic politics, not because it can guarantee any particular political outcome or ensure any particular political principle, but because it constitutes us as individuals able to live with the uncertainty that is at the heart of democratic politics.

Using performativity as a lens through which to analyze the practice of making rights claims requires a kind of dual vision. It requires that we take up the role of spectator and assume a capacity to distance ourselves from the thing being described. In the process of exploring and describing the practice of rights claiming, we render it a somewhat static object, at least temporarily. We then obfuscate, again temporarily, the fact that what we describe is continually being remade, and gloss over the fact that we, as spectators, are participants in that process of construction and reconstruction, that how we describe something is part of the production of the thing itself. The challenge is to balance the treatment of rights claiming as a specific thing with a treatment of it as an ongoing activity in which spectators are co-participants in the creation and recreation of the very thing under examination. This means treating rights claiming as a linguistic practice, a gamelike activity that has rules or conventions that can be acknowledged, enforced, and observed, but are, nonetheless, never wholly comprehensive, permanently fixed, or even always completely identifiable. Games—whether they are language games, sports games, cards games, or even politics—are always played by individuals who have the creative capacity to change the rules as they play, by people who are simultaneously embedded in a linguistic community and yet creators of that community, shaped by language and reshaping language through its use.[34]

A Sketch of the Book

The book unfolds in two parts. In the first part (Chapters Two and Three) I use various concepts from speech act theory to engage the arguments in key philosophical works on rights, while in the second half (Chapters Four and Five) I turn my attention more directly to an analysis of rights politics. Those interested in illustrations of how a performative analysis reveals the democratic character of certain contemporary rights-based political efforts might choose to begin with the discussion of same-sex marriage debates in Chapter Four or the AIDS policy analysis in Chapter Five. Chapters Two and Three, of course, provide the theoretical background to this political analysis and offer brief engagement with several historical examples of rights politics as a means of illustration.

In these early chapters, I shed light on and offer an alternative to what I contend is a dominant way of thinking about what rights are and do that limits our understanding of their democratic character. I use the speech act theory distinction between illocutionary and perlocutionary utterances to show that a good deal of contemporary rights scholarship—particularly that which is concerned about rights' ontological underpinnings and political effects—is preoccupied with the idea that rights are, can, or should be "trumps"—that is, felicitous speech acts that have clear rules that, if followed correctly, will bring political disputes to a clear and predictable end. Here, I work with and against the arguments of scholars such as Ronald Dworkin, Mary Ann Glendon, and Michael Ignatieff to explore the implications that a rights-as-trumps conception has for democratic theory and practice. In Chapter Three, I argue that we would be better off understanding rights as perlocutionary utterances, and in particular, claims of persuasion, than as illocutionary utterances that trump. Working with insights drawn from the unlikely sources of Hannah Arendt and John Stuart Mill, I argue that understanding what rights are and do in terms of the perlocutionary practice of persuasion entails a more robust appreciation of language and linguistic being than a rights-as-trumps conception and generates an orientation to politics far more conducive to the demands of democracy in the twenty-first century. Indeed, moving from an understanding of rights claims as illocutionary utterances that trump to thinking about them as perlocutionary utterances of persuasion, allows us to envision both the subject of rights and the practice of rights politics anew, moving us beyond the familiar impasse of either defending or criticizing rights for their promotion and protection of individualistic concerns. Indeed, it even helps us to see John Stuart Mill less as a theorist of an individualistic approach to rights and more as someone who embraced and advanced rights claiming as an uncertain but nonetheless important participatory democratic practice.

If what is often referred to as the liberal-communitarian debates about rights form the backdrop against which Chapters Two and Three are written, the critical theory and Left legal debates about rights form the backdrop for Chapters Four and Five. In Chapter Four, for example, I take up the concern that making rights claims on behalf of members of particular identity groups may reinforce pernicious identity categories and undermine rather than advance democratic values and practices. Focusing my attention on the debate over same-sex marriage rights in California, I show how and why rights claiming remains a valuable democratic practice even when the claims themselves seem to reinforce normative categories of identity. More specifically, I illuminate the ways in which rights claiming provides an opportunity to contest, reimagine, and enact different practices of good citizenship. I draw attention to how this is done through rights claims made on both sides of the issue, thereby highlighting the fact that the performativity of rights claiming is neither necessarily tied up with progressive political aims nor always consistent across any one side of a debate. Indeed, the same-sex marriage debates show us clearly that the persuasive and performative nature of any single rights claim is, itself, quite complex and always just one small part of a politics of ongoing political engagement. At the same time, however, these debates, and particularly the claim for a right to marry members of the same sex, offer insight into the transformative potential of rights claiming. It is through this particular rights claim, I argue, that the boundaries and meaning of responsible citizenship are challenged and reformed.

If to make claims like "The people have a right to self-governance" or "Gays and lesbians have a right to marry" is not to hold the winning card that will shut down debate once and for all but is, rather, to engage in an activity with others that has multiple effects and outcomes that are beyond my control, what makes rights claiming a particularly democratic practice? If Chapter Four answers that question by suggesting that rights claiming provides a language through which we articulate and enact, at times even transform, our understandings of whom we are as citizens and a community, Chapter Five takes this insight further. Here, I show how rights claiming allows previously marginalized individuals to take part in the important practice of speaking and acting in public and to create new forms of political subjectivity. Exploring rights claims made in response to particular AIDS policies advanced in both the United States and South Africa, I argue that the democratic potential of rights claiming lies not necessarily in the laws or politics it engenders or in bringing closure to a particular political debate but in the fact that it allows individuals silenced by illness, class, race, and other factors to unite and engage in acts of democratic citizenship that shift the very meaning of democratic community.

In Chapter Six, I return more explicitly to some of the questions that inspired this text. As I argue here, attention to the performative dimensions of rights claiming will not answer many of the commonly asked questions about rights in ways that all will find satisfying. It does not tell us precisely how we should adjudicate competing rights claims, nor does it offer an alternative theory of rights that will prove to be irrefutable, thus guaranteeing particular political outcomes. The goal here is not to devise a framework that can account for all our assertions of rights nor to identify the underlying structure common to all rights claim. Such goals would be antithetical to the very understanding of politics and the performative dimensions of rights claiming that I outline in these pages. Instead, the aim of this book is to seek a more comprehensive understanding of what it is we are doing when we make a rights claim and how it is that we do what we do. If we have a better understanding of what we are doing when we make rights claims, we may be able to engage rights more effectively—or at least in ways that are more consistent with our intuitions about democracy.

2

Rights as Trumps and the Quest for Certainty

IN MAKING THE case for treating rights claims as performative utterances, and rights claiming as a performative practice, I do not mean to suggest that either the public discourse or the scholarly treatment of rights ignores their performativity altogether. Indeed, as I argue in this chapter, our everyday practice of and philosophical debates about rights claiming actually recognize—though often not explicitly or fully enough—the fact that rights claiming is a practice that shapes and changes our sense of self, our relationships to others, and the communities in which we live. Consider the following examples. Imagine that you are at a convention of the National Rifle Association (N.R.A.). You are a lifelong member of the N.R.A., an ardent supporter of the Second Amendment to the U.S. Constitution, and you are surrounded by like-minded people. Or imagine that you are at a pro-choice march in Washington, D.C., with a group of close friends who have been active in the fight for women's reproductive freedom for a number of years. What would it mean for you to say "I have a right to bear arms" at the convention or "Women have a right to privacy" at the march? Presumably everyone you are with knows that the law grants individuals these rights. They may recognize and worry that such rights are being challenged on a variety of fronts, but they agree with you that such rights do or should exist. It would seem, then, that to say "I have a right to X" would be to make a constative statement, to utter a simple fact about the world in which we live. Were you to make this claim to someone who disagreed with you, you might then go on to explain—using the law, moral reasoning, or philosophical argumentation—why it is that they are incorrectly understanding something about the world, and you would likely understand the conflict or dilemma as a failure on the other person's part to recognize a reality others can see, a truth others accept.

However, as speech act theory tells us, our utterances are never simply statements about the world, never purely constative utterances that are solely assessable or comprehensible in terms of their truth or falsity. Utterances are also actions and practices, often performative acts that bring new relationships and new ways of being into existence. To some extent, of course, your actions—indeed, your very presence—at the particular political event, already contains some recognition of this. To be sure, it is quite likely that the purpose of attending the convention or the march is to discuss and debate which philosophical, legal, or moral arguments might convince dissenters to see the world differently, and in such cases, you would not be wholly incorrect to treat your rights claims as constative utterances. At the same time, however, you are likely to recognize that no matter what arguments you marshal, it is doubtful that you will be able to convince everyone to agree with your understanding of which rights people do or should have. This will not necessarily lessen your willingness to make rights claims—to the general public, the scholarly community, or the judiciary; in fact, you may make rights claims precisely because you recognize the difficulty, if not the impossibility, of achieving complete agreement. You may make rights claims, that is, for quite different purposes: rather than to present a fact about the world, your activity may entail rallying your constituency or registering your disapproval of the government. Quite likely you will direct the claim to protestors in order to establish boundaries or differences between yourselves and those with whom you disagree, to shut their voices out, to take their perspective off the table, or to bring the debate to a clear and concise end. Doing this suggests that on some level you appreciate that rights claiming is, like any other speech act, always more than just a statement of facts; it is also a doing, an activity that shapes the world in which we live. You may be treating the rights claim as a constative statement when you think that those who disagree with you are simply misunderstanding the truth of the situation, and yet you appreciate the claim as a performative utterance to the extent that you expect that the making of the claim has an important and specific impact on the world and on others, even in the face of such disagreement.

An implicit recognition of the performativity of rights claiming can be found in philosophical definitions of rights, as well as our common intuitions and everyday usage. Take the classic definition offered by H. L. A. Hart: to say that "X has a right to p" is to make a corresponding claim about the duties or moral obligations of Y, in which case having a right justifies constraining the actions of another person or institution such that they do not infringe on X's enjoyment of *p*.[1] Traditionally, debates about the meaning and democratic implications of Hart's definition, as well as other understandings of rights, tend to revolve around whether the claim itself can be said to describe reality accurately—that is, whether X has a particular right that Y should respect or even whether *p* should be called a right at all. At the same time, a great deal of academic and general discourse on rights concerns itself with questions of what rights *are* (e.g., universal truths, cosmopolitan norms of morality, legal or political constructs) or with justifying the legal, political, or moral existence of particular rights and corresponding duties. Nonetheless, even traditional definitions of rights, much like the everyday practice of making such claims, reveals some surprising insights into the performative character of rights claiming. Indeed, Hart's definition reminds us that through the making of a rights claim, one sets the terms of a particular relationship. Though "I have a right to *p*" may not be as explicit a performative as the more traditional Austinian examples of "I bet" or "I do," it is still the case that *in* and *by* making the claim, the speaker changes the context in which he or she is embedded—a process that may include changing the relationships between individuals, shifting one's own sense of self, making possible or foreclosing certain political and social arrangements, and, of course, affecting the subjective states of listeners.[2]

In this chapter and the next, I bring this often implicit recognition of the performativity of rights to the fore in order to see what it reveals about our dominant understandings of the relationship between rights and democracy. That is, I read contemporary rights discourse with an eye toward what it suggests about the democratic character of rights claiming rather than what it suggests about the meaning or justification of a right; and I argue that while rights scholarship often recognizes some of the illocutionary or perlocutionary dimensions of the practice, it does not take the insights about performativity far enough. In fact, it often obscures the complexity and messiness of performative practices in ways that have a significant bearing on how we understand, or perhaps misunderstand, the democratic character of making rights claims.[3] To illuminate the contemporary yet partial recognition of rights claiming as a performative practice, I examine what has become perhaps the most common way of thinking about what rights are and do captured in the metaphor of *rights as trumps*.[4] To be sure, the notion of rights as trumps is closely associated with the work of legal scholar Ronald Dworkin and a particular set of ideas associated with liberal political theory and its ambivalence about majority decision making. And, of course, it has its share of critics. Not all scholars or activists agree that rights are correctly understood as trumps that are meant to place limits on the power of majorities, nor do they agree about whether trumping is consistent with democracy. Many are quite skeptical about whether or not rights can, do, or should function as trumps; and even when there is agreement that rights are and do trump other kinds of claims, there is often considerable debate about whether rights get their trumping power from a source beyond or within the confines of politics and society. Despite these disagreements, elements of a rights-as-trumps conception remain at the heart of analyses of rights' efficacy and democratic potential. This is particularly the case to the extent that rights scholars focus on how to make rights claims work to produce a particular outcome. In the language of performativity, this reflects a concern with identifying and perhaps fixing the felicity conditions of the claim or an effort to make visible and even stabilize the norms or conventions that are assumed to be essential to the successful working or "uptake" of the rights claim itself. My concern is that such a preoccupation with these felicity conditions—the rules of the game of rights claiming, so to speak—may mislead us about what makes rights claiming democratic.

This chapter thus makes three distinct but related points. First, I suggest that approaching the rights-as-trumps metaphor as an insight about the performativity of rights claiming sheds new light on its meaning and the debates surrounding it. In particular, it moves us beyond debates that assess the democratic character of rights in terms of their relationship to majority decision making. Second, I contend that the rights-as-trumps conception, a least in a modified form, is far more pervasive than we might think. It is not simply a metaphor embraced by thinkers closely identified with the liberal political tradition or who espouse an atomistic individualism; in fact, vestiges of it can be found in the writings of democratic theorists and others who seek to move beyond certain philosophical commitments associated with liberalism or natural rights theory. Third, I argue that a rights-as-trumps conception is both valuable and problematic, not because it rests on a particular understanding of the metaphysics and ontology of rights but, rather, because of what it reveals about our understanding and expectations of linguistic actors engaged in democratic politics. More specifically, I suggest that to the extent that we remain wedded exclusively to the conception of rights claiming as an activity that can or should bring political debate to a close, we embrace an unnecessarily narrow view of language concerned with identifying and fixing the felicity conditions of the speech act, and we advance a political ethos that compromises our capacity to be rights-bearing actors in democratic societies. Offering a performative conception of rights claiming that is more consistent with the demands of contemporary democratic politics is the project of chapter three.

Are Rights Trumps?

To say that "rights are trumps" is simultaneously to repeat a piece of conventional wisdom and to raise a topic of considerable dispute. Ronald Dworkin may have been the one to popularize the notion of rights-as-trumps when he suggested that "Individuals have rights when, for some reason, a collective goal is not a sufficient justification for denying them what they wish, as individuals, to have or to do, or not sufficient justification for imposing some loss or injury upon them."[5] And yet, the idea that rights have a special importance that preempts other considerations, often those of the majority, goes much further back and much further forward. Since at least the seventeenth century, and particularly within the liberal political tradition, rights language has signaled, as Jeremy Waldron explains, the limits to be placed on the scope of state power. They represent, in other words, those "interests and considerations that . . . would warrant overriding other values and ideals" in cases of conflict.[6] Such an understanding of rights—indeed, the very language of trumping—often appears in contemporary accounts of rights as well, whether these are journalistic or scholarly, activist or academic, critical or celebratory.[7] As a number of commentators have noted, human rights activists regularly depict rights as trumps, assuming that they will or should supersede arguments that rest on concerns about social utility, that they will or should shield individuals from various atrocities in ways that advance human freedom, and that they will or should "bring political disputes to closure and conclusion."[8] Even someone like Martha Nussbaum, more a proponent of a capabilities than a rights approach to justice, advances a trumplike understanding of rights when she describes them as "very urgent items that should be secured to people no matter what else we pursue" and that should function as "a system of side-constraints" on government practices and policies.[9]

The prevalence of the rights-as-trumps concept is, of course, quite controversial: debates abound about whether or not rights *are* trumps and about whether or not their trumping is good for democracy. As some critics point out, to the extent that rights are trumps, they are extraordinarily ineffective, rarely functioning to bring political debate to clear ends or reign in the power of democratic majorities.[10] Moreover, as others suggest, to the extent that they do work to constrain majoritarian decision making, trumping rights undermine the very essence of democracy—the self-government of the people. Still other critics argue that understanding rights as trump cards in the game of politics actually threatens the fabric of democratic community because its rests on a misconception of human nature and devalues the importance of social relationships. These critics often trace the rights-as-trumps notion back to the writings of John Locke, who is taken to argue that rights are a kind of property of discrete individuals that can and should be used to erect barriers between people and to shield them from the reach of the state. Such an understanding of rights as the property of atomistic individuals is said to obscure the fundamentally social and contextual dimensions of human subjectivity and produce a divisive and individualistic political ethos.[11] For example, as Mary Ann Glendon explains, when we think of rights as trumps, we see ourselves as lone individuals in conflict and competition with others. Relating to others in this way, she argues, engenders "a near-aphasia concerning responsibility" and threatens the very fabric of a healthy democracy to the extent that it "promote[s] unrealistic expectations, heighten[s] social conflict, and inhibit[s] dialogue that might lead toward consensus, accommodation, or at least the discovery of common ground."[12] What concerns Glendon about the relationship between rights and democracy is not that rights may be at odds with the decisions of democratically elected majorities, and certainly not that rights are ineffective political tools; for her, the problem with the rights-as-trumps conception is that it jeopardizes the very values that are necessary for sustaining robust democratic communities.[13]

I rehearse these likely familiar concerns about rights-as-trumps not to take a side in what is often referred to as the liberal-communitarian debate but, rather, to juxtapose the focus of these debates to an analysis that places questions of performativity at its center. Instead of trying to determine whether rights *are* trumps, or even whether rights-as-trumps are good for democracy, I explore what rights scholars think it means to liken the activity of claiming rights to the activity of trumping and thus investigate the practice of making rights trump in terms of its illocutionary and perlocutionary dimensions. In this chapter, I draw particular attention to the illocutionary dimensions of rights claiming, to how theories of rights presume that rights claims work and what they suggest it means for a rights claim to be successful or effective. In chapter three I focus more attention on the perlocutionary dimensions of rights claiming.

As I mentioned in the previous chapter, speech act theory draws our attention to the fact that our utterances are always a set of acts, one of which Austin calls the *illocutionary* act. This refers to what a speaker does *in* the process of saying something. To say "I am sorry," for example, is not to state a fact about the world that exists prior to the speaking, but to do the apologizing in the saying itself, just as to say "I do" in the course of a wedding ceremony is to engage in the activity of marrying. Of course, as Austin reminds us, for an illocutionary act to be successful—for "I'm sorry" to be an apology or "I do" to be a vow—it must be uttered under the appropriate circumstances and make reference to conventions that both exist and are acknowledged by others.[14] It is not enough, in other words, for a speaker to use a particular word or even intend a particular outcome for an utterance to work. The successful uptake of an illocutionary utterance requires that it be uttered in accordance with conventional procedures and with respect to conventional effects: it must meet a variety of felicity conditions.[15] This is true whether we are talking about a political practice or a game of cards.

In a game of cards, to play a trump is to play a card that wins a hand. Of course, whether a particular card such as the jack of spades or the ace of diamonds is a trump has nothing to do with the value of the card itself but, rather, with the agreed-upon rules of the game. The act of throwing down the card and, at least figuratively, saying "I trump you," wins or trumps only if it meets the felicity conditions of the game. In other words, I may have had a particular card in my hand, but it is in the act of throwing the card down that I do the activity and to a certain extent create the thing I seem to be describing—but only in a particular context. Just as saying "I do" on stage during a play does not marry me to another person, throwing a jack of spades during a game of Ping-Pong does not make me the winner. Likewise, if I throw down the jack of spades during a game of Euchre when diamonds are trump, my utterance will fail. In order for the throwing of a particular card to function successfully as a trump, it must reference certain social norms or, in the language of games, follow certain rules. For example, all the players must recognize that they are playing a game in which a distinct card or suit has a greater power than others, and they must agree that when the card is thrown at the correct time, it beats another card. These established rules, usually agreed upon at least implicitly, not only help us determine what suit or which card in a particular suit beats other cards but also tell us when and by whom a trump card can be thrown, as well as what happens as a result of its throwing. These rules are the social norms or conventions that form the background against which we play, informing not only how we act but also how we understand ourselves and our relation to others: it is both the rules and our activities in the context of these conventions that make it possible for us to be partners or dealers, winners or losers.

To the extent that rights claiming is likened to trumping, it too is a practice with a set of rules, an understanding of the proper end or goal of play, and a notion of what makes one a winner or loser. Traditionally, as I suggested earlier, when we call rights "trumps," we often think of them as representing or reflecting eternal truths or universal agreements about what should be considered especially important to a society—so important that these considerations should take precedence over other concerns. Like the card of a particular suit that "takes" cards of other suits and thus wins the hand or the game, a rights claim serves as trump when and because it overrides another political argument and prevents (or should prevent) the implementation of policies and practices that advance competing priorities. Within a democratic context, trumping usually, though by no means necessarily, entails constraining the decisions of democratic majorities—particularly when those decisions would advance the general interests at the expense of individual freedom.[16] This commonsensical understanding of the rights-as-trumps conception certainly draws our attention to who wins or loses in the activity of rights claiming, but it tells us very little about the rules of the game. We do not learn, that is, what makes the rights claim work to trump or, exactly, what it means to win. That is what a performative analysis of rights theorizing can make visible.

Consider how a performative perspective shifts the way we read Ronald Dworkin's arguments. Quite often Dworkin is read as advancing a decidedly liberal conception of rights and the rights-bearing subject, and this leads critics to take him to task for misrepresenting what rights are, as well as for misunderstanding the human condition.[17] Reading Dworkin's work with an eye toward what it suggests about the performativity of rights claiming, however, allows us to get outside of these debates. Indeed, it allows us to put aside the question of whether or not Dworkin is a particular kind of *liberal* legal theorist while opening up the space to ask questions about what he thinks a rights claim does and how it does that successfully. Placing questions of performativity at the center of our analysis, in other words, highlights the extent to which Dworkin defends rights out of a concern that states and individuals are making incorrect choices about their priorities. Moreover, it draws our attention to the fact that he believes that these choices, tending as they do to privilege the common good over individual liberty interests, are actually at odds with the accepted, though perhaps somewhat forgotten, conventions, intuitions, or underlying commitments of democratic societies. His project, we can now see, is to make these conventions visible and to show how and when the utterance of a rights claim cites these conventions and thus should effectively end debate in favor of individual liberty. Merely saying "I have a right" in order to protect yourself from government interference does not mean the claim will or should override other considerations or bring a political dispute to an end. For a rights claims to be felicitous—in order for it to take precedence "over some background justification for political decisions that states a goal for the community as a whole"—it must be made under the proper circumstances.[18] These circumstances include the necessity that a rights claim reflect something of special interest to individuals rather than to groups, that it be spoken in the context of debates about what governments can and cannot do, and that it be spoken to people who are supposed to understand that the rights claim itself is more important than claims about the common good or general welfare. Speakers and listeners must recognize that the rights claim should properly trump utilitarian calculations to the extent that it advances a commitment to equality and egalitarianism, and this means that a successful trumping claim requires not only that the speaker cites the proper conventions but also that the listener acknowledges and agrees to these rules. This reading is not meant as a defense of Dworkin's account of the felicity conditions of rights claiming; indeed, there are many rights scholars who offer compelling reasons to think he has incorrectly identified the reasons a rights claim does or should work, as well as what it is we should expect a rights claim to do in the first place.[19] Nonetheless, we can read Dworkin's argument, as well as those that challenge or extend it, as an account of the performativity of rights claiming and, more specifically, of the felicity conditions of rights. In doing so, we can see that theories and conceptions of rights reveal far more than a correct or incorrect understanding of human nature or rights themselves.

We can, of course, engage in a similar performative analysis of rights scholarship that explicitly rejects the language of trumping. Here I am thinking of contemporary rights scholarship that embraces a "political" conception of rights or that is based on a deliberative approach to democratic politics. In this body of scholarship the use of the term "political" is meant to distinguish a particularly contextualized and historicized understanding of rights from a more metaphysical conception. Contemporary scholars who use the term "political" do not necessarily reject but, rather, bracket the search for metaphysical grounding, suggesting instead that we understand rights claims as political because of the important role they play in political life and because they get some of their meaning from their place in public debate and deliberation or when they accord with standards of public reason.[20] Treating rights claims as political in this sense, as well as placing them within the context of a practice of deliberative politics, however, does not necessarily mean that these scholars treat rights claims differently in terms of their performativity. In fact, we can see that, implicit in some important contemporary accounts of rights that eschew the idea that rights are trumps, there remains a tendency to treat rights claims as illocutionary utterances and thus a tremendous investment in identifying, as well as trying to fix, the conditions that make rights capable of bringing debate to an end.

I argue that this concern with identifying the felicity conditions of a rights claim and determining what a felicitous claim looks like is evidence of a modified version of the rights-as-trumps conception. Though contemporary rights scholars may reject the term *trump*, they retain a concern with what will make a rights claim win a particular political debate. This suggests that just as the trump card or suit can change in a game of cards (as can the very rules or conditions under which trumping is legitimate), rights claiming as a trumping activity can take a variety of forms and circulate under different names. In other words, to the extent that rights scholars are concerned with making rights claims effective at constraining government action or protecting individual freedom, I am suggesting that they can be said to be concerned with the trumping capacity of rights. They may describe this trumping in terms of making an effective or successful rights claim, and they may further specify that an efficacious rights claim is one that generates "reasoned loyalty" and establishes "a secure intellectual standing."[21] They may alternatively suggest that effective rights claims result from improved procedural or institutional mechanisms of engagement and enforcement or from the creation of a list of rights both comprehensive enough to ensure the well-being of individuals around the globe and general enough to garner acceptance across cultures and communities.[22] But despite such differences, these arguments share a concern with defining the efficacy of a right claim, and by defining this success of a claim in such narrow terms, they reinforce the idea that rights claiming is a trumping activity.

We find such a tendency in Michael Ignatieff's very provocative and influential *Human Rights as Politics and Idolatry*. Ignatieff states quite explicitly that he does not believe that rights are or should be understood as trumps if by trumps we mean claims that get their authority from some pre- or nonpolitical moral source. In fact, from his perspective, it is much more realistic and politically beneficial to recognize that rights get their meaning and power from the always messy processes of political compromise. According to Ignatieff, then, if we understand and embrace the idea that rights are political claims, part of a language that represents different and often competing perspectives, then we can appreciate that making rights claims is a practice that involves "painful compromises not only between means and ends, but between ends themselves" and recognize that "it is an illusion to suppose that the function of human rights is to define a higher realm of shared moral values that will assist contending parties to find common ground."[23] To be sure, then, Ignatieff rejects the idea that rights represent eternal verities, and he gestures toward an embrace of the idea that the outcomes of rights claiming, like any speech act, may not be controllable in advance of the complicated engagements of individuals. However, if we consider Ignatieff's argument in light of the categories and questions of performativity, we can see that he does not reject the idea that rights claiming can bring debate to a guaranteed end as wholly as he first seems to. In fact, he holds fast to a faith in the power of conventions to help us control the illocutionary force of a rights claim when he offers a definition of a successful or efficacious claim. A rights claim that meets the proper felicity conditions will generate "a common framework, a common set of reference points that can assist parties in conflict to deliberate together."[24] When rights claims do this successfully, they can achieve what Ignatieff believes is the ultimate goal of rights politics—providing a vision of life upon which all individuals would be able to agree. If a rights claim provides "a definition of the minimum conditions for any kind of life at all," it will, he suggests, "command universal assent."[25]

A concern with what makes a rights claim successful crops up in the work of Amartya Sen as well. Like Ignatieff, Sen rejects the idea that rights reflect some eternal truth about the world and thus challenges the idea that their trumping power comes from something outside of the political process. Instead, he suggests that rights come to have meaning only through the process of public debate and scrutiny, and he goes so far as to acknowledge that rights claiming rarely leads to any kind of political finality. Public discussion and scrutiny of rights claims, he explains, "leave room for further discussions, disputations and arguments," and thus while rights claiming may bring some debates and controversies to a conclusion, it will likely "leave others, at least tentatively, unsettled."[26] Here, then, Sen seems to be rejecting not only the traditional description of rights as trumps but also the very idea that the point of rights claiming is to trump. However, Sen refuses to allow this appreciation of the complexity, variation, or contingency of any practice of rights claiming to undermine a fundamental commonality he finds at the heart of rights theory and practice. Internal variation and deliberation sit comfortably alongside "the commonality of the agreed principle of attaching substantial importance to human rights (and to the corresponding freedoms and obligations) and of being committed to considering seriously how that importance should be appropriately reflected."[27] In other words, Sen's argument suggests that if we make rights claims in the correct way, under the proper circumstances (and if it is clear that we all understand and agree upon what these circumstances or rules are), we should be able to generate conclusions that "demand" a level of respect and acceptance. Sen may recognize that rights claiming is a complicated performative activity, but this recognition does not get him out of the logic of a rights-as-trumps conception. Indeed, to the extent that he attempts to define the outcome of a rights claim, he reduces the claim to an illocutionary utterance; and similarly, to the extent that he tries to determine precisely what makes it succeed, he reinforces the idea that language is a tool over which we, as speakers, have significant control. Sen's emphasis on commonality and proper procedures reflects both a concern with identifying felicity conditions and an attempt to stabilize a potentially unruly practice. He suggests, then, that however politically constructed or contingent a rights claim may be, if the proper rules of the game of rights claiming are followed, the correct people will win and freedom will be safeguarded.

My point in drawing attention to those places where Sen and Ignatieff evidence a clear desire for making (as well as suggestions about how to make) rights claims work is to suggest that this reflects a very particular, and particularly narrow, understanding of the performativity of rights claiming—one that unnecessarily reduces rights claims to illocutionary utterances that are to be evaluated by their successful uptake or their ability to bring about a clear and stable conclusion to a political controversy of some kind. While arguments such as Ignatieff's and Sen's may relocate the trumping capacity of rights claims from the make-up of the right itself to the procedures in and through which the rights claim is articulated, they nonetheless continue to treat the claim itself as a means to an end and rights claiming as a rule-bound practice that can be mastered.[28]

The Seductiveness and Costs of Felicity

The power of the modified conception of rights-as-trumps that I find in work like Ignatieff's and Sen's should not be underestimated. Given the many instances of injustice and inequality around the globe, and the long-held belief that rights can and should enable human freedom and flourishing, it is not surprising that there is interest in trying to identify, and even entrench, the procedures and conventions that would make rights claims successful illocutions. That we, as actors and scholars, want rights to work in particular ways, and that we seek to discover what precisely enables rights to trump, makes a great deal of sense on both a political and a practical level: who would not want to find a way to end practices of torture and abuse or to ensure human freedom and flourishing once and for all? Who wants to fight again and again to protect a freedom a person thought he or she had already won? We want the best argument to convince others and we want to guarantee effective enforcement of rights, especially since people's lives often depend on it. In some cases, perhaps the best cases, rights claiming does just that.

But as seductive or commonsensical as such a perspective might seem, conceiving of rights claiming as a trumping activity does not capture the whole picture of what we do in the process of making rights claims. Moreover, this way of thinking about what rights are and do actually limits our ability to understand the democratic character—the potential and the problems—of rights. Let me explain these limits by way of illustrating how a rights-as-trumps conception colors our understanding of rights practice. Imagine a group of individuals (tied together perhaps by ethnicity, religion, or political ideals) who have been politically disenfranchised from a particular nation-state and abused in numerous ways through either the actions or the inaction of a governing group. Now, imagine that such stateless people or refugees make claims for a right such as the right to political asylum or the right to freedom from torture, but their claims go unheeded, and no country takes the refugees in or intervenes on their behalf to prevent further atrocities. Their rights claims, it would seem, turn out to be anything but successful trumping claims in times of political crisis, and this despite what is likely widespread agreement on the presence of an injustice. There are a number of different ways one could understand rights claiming in a situation such as this if we think that rights are trumps. One could argue, for example, that the failure of rights claiming to protect these people from harm or to promote their dignity as human beings reveals the philosophical and political bankruptcy of the very idea of a right as a trump; whether rights are called human or natural, political or social, a rights claim that exceeds the bounds of the nation-state is nonsensical. We could say, particularly if we are attuned to the performativity of language, that the utterance fails because the felicity conditions of rights claiming were not met: either those who claimed rights had no standing because they were not citizens of a nation or they used the wrong language to fight tyranny and injustice. The implication here would be that, in order to advance democratic values and practices, it would be necessary to adopt alternative languages and strategies of political reform. If, however, we thought that it was proper to make claims to rights irrespective of one's status as a citizen, we might say that the claims failed to be secure uptake because the stateless did not follow the proper procedures, cite the correct conventions, or meet the conditions necessary to make a claim such as "We have a right to live without fear for our lives" felicitous. In other words, we would explain the infelicity of the claims by suggesting that the refugees addressed the claims to the wrong body or phrased their claims in ways that could not be understood by others. Additionally, we might attribute the failure of the claim to problems with the conventions or rules of the game themselves. Indeed, this is, to some extent, the interpretation implicit in attempts to create new declarations, procedures, or adjudicating bodies to ensure the proper reception and enforcement of rights claims. Attempts to fix the system by which rights claims are made, heard, and enforced can be seen, in other words, as efforts to change or clarify the very conventions or rules of the practice of rights claiming. There are, no doubt, distinctly different and plausible explanations for the failure of a rights claim to bring about a specific change in political or social practice. But what if we were to read these events from a different perspective, one that recognizes that linguistic performativity is not exhausted by the illocutionary dimensions of an utterance—if, in other words, we expanded our understanding of performativity beyond the narrow confines of instrumentality? We might then see that what is a failure on one front is actually quite productive on many others. For example, we might see that the language of rights brought a group of people together who would otherwise have had little reason to join forces, or we might find that claiming rights produced a shift in ways of thinking about citizenship or statehood that were not captured in legal terms. It would certainly lead to a shift in understandings of the power of rights claiming going forward.[29] I will explore effects such as these in greater depth in the coming chapters. Here, let me explain the philosophical and political motivation for questioning the value of thinking about rights as trumps.

A rights-as-trumps conception, I am arguing, is problematic because it does not fully acknowledge the complexity of linguistic performativity and thus gives rise to an orientation toward political engagement that can be troubling. The problem with the rights-as-trumps conception is neither that it poses rights as constraints on the behavior of democratic majorities nor that it advances a particularly individualistic and antagonistic ethos: rights claiming may do both, or neither, at any one time. Instead, the problem is that a rights-as-trumps conception presents rights claiming as an activity that can and should bring debate to an end by producing clear and secure winners. This way of understanding what it means to make rights claims obscures the fact that the practice is, like all speech activity, fundamentally unpredictable and always changing, and it reinforces the idea (perhaps the fantasy) that we can have complete sovereignty over language and political outcomes. Efforts to identify the felicity conditions of a rights claim or the desire to end a political debate are not unwarranted or unreasonable; nonetheless, they should not obscure the fact that making rights trump is always a fraught activity.

Indeed, a number of important contemporary theories of linguistic being and democratic politics take issue with precisely the emphasis on determining the felicity conditions of engagement that even a modified version of the rights-as-trumps conception perpetuates. As theories of language remind us, it is extremely difficult to control fully the outcomes of one's speech acts, no matter how well conventions are cited or how accurately felicity conditions are met. The contingency of any speech act is a result, in part, of the fact that we, as speaking beings, never have a purely instrumental relationship to language; we can never fully know or communicate our intentions to others, nor can listeners grasp these intentions completely.[30] We are speaking subjects who not only use but also are ourselves the products of language; we are embedded in linguistic communities along with others with whom we communicate. Language thus serves as the background against which we speak as well as the medium through we constitute ourselves as individual, though it neither fully determines who we are and what we can do nor enables sovereignty or complete control over the effects of its use.

Interestingly enough, insights into the ambiguities of linguistic subjectivity, and thus communication, are not always embraced by theorists associated with speech act theory. Indeed, an important strand of speech act theory focuses primarily on mapping the meanings and rules of language in an effort to achieve not only clarity about meaning but also mastery of effect. A recognition of the contingency and complexity of linguistic activity thus calls into question one of the fundamental impulses of speech act theory: the effort to offer a precise mapping of all speech activity accompanied by the illumination of those felicity conditions that make illocutionary acts successful. To assume or expect that we can determine, in advance, precisely what makes an utterance work is to forget not only that every utterance is actually a variety of speech activities but also that the quest for felicity may be quite futile. Indeed, these are some of the insights offered up by a version of speech act theory associated with a postfoundationalist philosophical approach. For example, as someone like Derrida argues, Austin may be incorrect to suggest that for an illocutionary act to have been performed it must have been performed successfully. It may actually be the case that illocutionary "failure" is a constitutive part of all linguistic activity and thus does not indicate the lack of an important speech activity. In fact, that an utterance does not succeed in engendering a particular effect may not be a reflection of some "failure" on the part of the speaker to cite the proper conventions or of the listener to recognize them but, rather, of the fact that "conventions" themselves are impossible to pin down. Though a written or spoken sign, even a bodily gesture, may seem to reference some social norm or convention—and thus appear to be a citation or copy of some original rule—it is never an exact replication, according to Derrida, because there is no precise original. Moreover, even when utterances repeat what we take to be agreed upon conventions and norms, the effects of the claims are still open to uncertainty, as utterances can be misheard or misinterpreted by those to whom they are directed.

Repeated utterances can also be used out of the originally intended context and, as a result, radically alter the effect or force of the utterance itself.[31] For example, to use a word such as *marriage* to refer to a relationship not sanctioned by the state may be to dislodge common ways of thinking and acting such that new forms of being and doing are opened up.

Recognizing these gaps between speech and effect, in turn, has a significant bearing on how we understand the democratic character and implications of communication. If we accept that the messiness of language is a general feature of linguistic activity, we must also recognize that it is an essential element of political life—of the practice of speaking and acting together. This is, in part, what motivates a democratic theorist such as Michael Walzer to challenge political scholars and actors to acknowledge the contingency and instability of political outcomes, and to embrace a new kind of political ethos. Because "permanent settlements are rare in political life," it makes more sense, he suggests, to understand political activity as "the endless return to these disagreements and conflicts, the struggle to manage and contain them and, at the same time, [the desire] to win whatever temporary victories are available."[32] Chantal Mouffe and Bonnie Honig reinforce this message when they call into question the equation of the political sphere with state institutions and political efficacy with the absence of conflict. As Mouffe argues, politics and political success cannot be captured by the administrative operations or "technical moves and neutral procedures" of the state.[33] Honig also suggests that the very project of political theory needs to be rethought so that it takes seriously the contingency of politics, rather than always seeking "to resolve institutional questions, to get politics right, over and done with, to free modern subjects and their sets of arrangements of political conflict and instability."[34] Political theorists who define politics in these ways do so not only to offer a more accurate description of the activity in which we are engaged but also to make a point about the orientation we should take toward political engagement. While an understanding of politics that calls into question the possibility of final outcomes may be worrisome to some, these thinkers suggest that it is only through the fundamentally uncertain and unstable practice of engaging with others that we create what Hannah Arendt calls "the world in common." Contemporary democratic theorists argue that we should recognize politics as a practice of acting and speaking with others and appreciate that the value of this practice resides less in its outcomes than in simply its doing. I follow such thinkers in their exhortation to understand politics in this way—to appreciate the importance of cultivating an orientation to politics that embraces unpredictability and fosters practices of discussion, persuasion, and often disagreement. Such an understanding of democratic politics, moreover, emphasizes the riskiness and the promise, the open-endedness and the transformative outcomes, of such engagement.

The political ethos that these theorists recommend recognizes and even embraces the tensions between instrumentalism and contingency, between political agency and indeterminacy. Thus, this kind of ethos has affinities with, and at times quite explicitly builds on, speech act theory. Indeed, if we take seriously the fact that language is more than a representation of an already existing reality, and understand it as something we use together that has effects on and for us that are often beyond our control, then we can no longer think about the claims we make as separate from the politics in which we engage nor can we consider language simply as a tool to be used in a political struggle. Recognizing the intersubjective and contingent dimensions of language means complicating any notion of political activity as the instrumental effort of a particular person or group to bring about a particular end. It thus calls into question if not the effort to identify then certainly the effort to fix the felicity conditions of a speech activity. Such insights unfortunately get lost in some of the compelling accounts of the political character of rights offered in recent years.

If taking the performativity of right claims to heart requires recognizing the multiple activities in which we engage when we make rights claims, it may also require letting go of the idea that we can guarantee the success of rights claims. We may need to give up on or at least loosen our attachment to the need for identifying and correcting for specific felicity conditions. Indeed, it may be the case that what look like the failures of rights claiming turn out to be the conditions of their political performativity. Too much attention to the problem of trumping or to determining the intellectual or institutional conditions that would ensure the successful uptake of a rights claim may actually obscure other aspects of its democratic potential. Too much emphasis on using rights in order to end a political controversy or disagreement or to achieve commonality may actually cultivate an orientation toward or ethos of political engagement that threatens to displace politics itself.[35] The conception of rights-as-trumps is problematic, then, not because it is empirically or even politically flawed but, rather, because it unnecessarily narrows our understanding of the relationship between rights and democracy, clouding our recognition of the democratic potential of rights claiming while downplaying the political limits of the practice itself. To put the point differently, a focus on rights claiming as a trumping activity obscures important aspects of performativity, having to do with the messy or uncontrollable elements of speech activity. Obscuring the fact that the effects of speech activities are never wholly under the control of a sovereign subject has a significant bearing on how we understand or perhaps misunderstand the democratic character of making rights claims. As I suggest in the next chapter, a fuller appreciation of the democratic character of rights requires that we think of rights as perspectival claims and rights claiming as a practice of persuasion.

3

Rights Claiming as a Practice of Persuasion

AS I ARGUED in the previous chapter, reexamining some of our common intuitions and contemporary arguments about rights claiming from the perspective of performativity reveals that the rights-as-trumps conception is more pervasive than we might have first thought. It is also troubling for reasons other than those we might have expected. A conception of rights-as-trumps is a problem for democracy and democratic theory not because it misrepresents human nature, perpetuates a litigious individualism, or fails to accurately reflect what a right *is*, as critics often suggest, but, rather, because it overemphasizes the possibility, perhaps even the importance, of defining and determining the success of a rights claim.[1] To the extent that we think of and theorize rights as trumps of any kind, we unnecessarily narrow our understanding of the performative dimensions of rights claiming and focus our attention on only (or only some of) the illocutionary dimensions of the practice. This tendency, expressed in a preoccupation with mapping out the felicity conditions of rights claiming, not only obscures other important aspects of language use and linguistic being but also undermines efforts to cultivate a political ethos suited to the demands of contemporary democracy. In this chapter I offer a performative conception of rights claiming that is more attentive to the complexities of language and the demands of democratic politics. I capture this by discussing rights claiming as a perlocutionary practice of persuasion, and I turn my attention to the work of Hannah Arendt and John Stuart Mill to elaborate.

If rights claiming is to be understood as a practice of persuasion rather than the act of throwing down a trump card, both Hannah Arendt and John Stuart Mill may seem unlikely thinkers from whom to draw inspiration. Arendt is famous for what appears to be a devastating critique that highlights the futility of rights claims made in the early part of the twentieth century, and John Stuart Mill is considered by many to be a champion of precisely the conception of rights-as-trumps I questioned in the previous chapter.[2] However, as I suggest in the pages to come, such readings may be too quick to pigeonhole these thinkers, one as a critic and the other a champion of a particular kind of rights. Reading their writings together, and with attention to their insights about the performativity of language and its implications for democratic politics, I suggest that both thinkers embrace a more complicated understanding of rights claiming—one that sheds light on both the promise and the limits of the practice for the creation and re-creation of democratic community.

Making Claims of Persuasion

To call rights claiming an act of persuasion and to promote persuasion as an important democratic practice rests on a particular definition of persuasion. After spending some time on the outskirts, perhaps even in the trash bin of democratic theory, "persuasion" has made something of a comeback in recent years. Like a number of the other terms under discussion in this book, however, the frequent use of the term "persuasion" should not be mistaken for its having a single meaning or a common emphasis. Bryan Garsten, for example, rescues the term from its negative association with practices of political manipulation and deceit, in part, by revealing the important place it has had in the history of democratic theory; and contemporary theorists of deliberative democracy are suggesting, more and more, that persuasion is a key aspect of any politics committed to the equality of persons and legitimate outcomes.[3] However, for some like Garsten, persuasion is a practice that, when understood properly, engages both sentiments and reason in ways that make it possible for us to connect with others. For others, persuasion is often defined, at least implicitly, as a purely logical activity that leads another person to change his or her mind. In Garsten's case, persuasion is an activity that explicitly eschews force or coercive power, while in the latter case, such power is often precisely persuasion's political virtue. Further confusing things, the term itself can refer either to the act of persuading or to fact of having been persuasive, and this ambiguity then leads to the question of whether one can be engaged in persuasion and yet fail to be persuasive, be persuasive without persuading. If, however, we think about persuasion from the perspective of a robust understanding of the performativity of language, we might be able to avoid such confusions.

Claims of persuasion, J. L. Austin's brief discussion on the topic tells us, are best understood as perlocutionary utterances rather than illocutionary ones. This means, as I mentioned in chapter one, that utterances meant to persuade have "effects" rather than a particular "force," as well as the considerable possibility of gaps between the words spoken and the resulting effects. This is due, in part, to the fact that perlocutions are decidedly "unconventional" speech acts. Their performativity is not a result of their having met a set of felicity conditions nor would one categorize the effect of a perlocutionary utterance as a "successful uptake" or "felicity." In fact, there is no formula by which we can capture what precisely happens *by* the making of a persuasive (or other perlocutionary) utterance because it is not determined, or at least not dependent upon, the speaker having cited appropriate norms.

This means that the outcomes of perlocutionary utterances like claims of persuasion are unpredictable and contingent: what happens *by* rather than *in* the utterance is quite outside the realm of the speaker's control and quite separate from the whole of the performative force of the claim. This does not, however, make a perlocutionary utterance any less an important performative speech act to recognize and appreciate; it simply makes it a distinct kind of speech activity. It is distinct because it engages the affective dimensions of human subjectivity—because it influences, and even constitutes, the way a speaker or listener feels. In addition, a perlocutionary utterance involves the speaker's sharing his or her perspective on the world, imagining the perspectives of others, and recognizing that one's utterance may or may not have the desired effect on others' behavior. For example, when I shout "Fire!" in order to warn someone about an impending danger (an illocutionary utterance), I may also be trying to scare the person and persuade him or her to flee the building. While my utterance will likely warn the person if I have said it according to the proper conventions—that is, if I have met the appropriate felicity conditions of warning—the emotional impact of my utterance is beyond my control. I may think that "Fire!" will trigger fear because it would for me, and I imagine that you and I would feel similarly in the case of impending danger, but my utterance may trigger a sense of heroism in you that I could only admire rather than understand. That someone may be persuaded to flee the building while others are persuaded to run into the building are both effects that I must accept if I understand what I am doing *by* making such a claim. The point here is that the effect of a claim of persuasion is not something that can be controlled through the application of rules; its "effectiveness" can neither be taught nor perfected, as

Danielle Allen notes.[4] It is, however, precisely this contingency and affectivity that make perlocutionary utterances, like claims of persuasion, important forms of political speech.

To explain what it means to recognize persuasion as a perlocutionary act that has an important place in a democratic politics, Hannah Arendt's work is helpful. Though Arendt is clearly writing before the advent of what has come to be known as "speech act theory," Arendt the agonistic democrat reveals a great appreciation for the constitutive or generative activity that is the practice of speaking to and communicating with others. She is, of course, well known for celebrating and promoting active engagement with others in the public realm as central to both the meaning and the possibility of democratic freedom; and she is known, though not always celebrated, for suggesting that this engagement involves—indeed, cannot and should not try to eradicate—discord, conflict, and uncertainty of outcomes. This makes her vision of democratic politics quite distinct from more traditional or dominant understandings of the properly democratic or political. Her understanding of politics calls into question the belief that political speech and activity are purely or solely means to an end and challenges the idea that freedom is the state of being unencumbered by or unengaged with others. What is less well established about Arendt's vision is that it takes the practice of persuasion, a practice that is decidedly perlocutionary, as a quintessential component of political activity.

As readers familiar with Arendt know, she bases her vision of politics and democratic freedom on the political practices of ancient Greece, or rather, a very particular moment in ancient Greece that precedes Plato's writing of the *Republic*. According to Arendt, the Greeks of Socrates' time and before understood political activity as a practice of exchanging views or opinions with others, a practice they called *peithein* and which Arendt translates roughly as "persuasion." *Peithein*, Arendt explains, entailed the sharing of one's opinion (*doxa*) or way of seeing the world with one's fellow citizens, with the expectation that one would be exposed to their perspectives in turn. On this account, to make a claim in the political realm meant to discuss and to debate one's understanding or view of the world (*dokei moi*) while listening to and learning from the views of others.[5] Arendt is drawn to this vision of politics because of its fundamental recognition of the plurality or distinctiveness of individuals as well as its faith in people's capacity to make judgments for themselves. *Peithein*, which Arendt identifies as "the highest, the truly political art," not only recognizes and embraces the fact that different individuals have distinct perspectives on the world but also appreciates that the point of political activity is to have the opportunity to present and debate these different takes on the world rather than to determine whose perspective is necessarily the correct one.[6] The early Greeks understood that acting and speaking in public, engaging in politics, were neither equivalent to nor measured by one's ability to ensure that a particular outcome resulted from one's utterance. Instead, they valued claims making in the public realm for the opportunities it provided, not the outcomes it promised: "To assert one's own opinion belonged to being able to show oneself, to be seen and heard by others. To the Greeks this was the one great privilege attached to public life."[7] The privilege to be savored is the opportunity to *act* persuasively, not the guarantee of *having been* persuasive, and this opportunity is an essential component of human freedom, as Arendt sees it. While Greeks valued the fact, in other words, that "the world opens up differently . . . according to [an individual's] position in it,"[8] Arendt values the fact that the Greeks refused to reduce the importance of political engagement to successfully persuading or convincing another to see the world from their point of view.

For those in need of a more robust answer to the question "Why participate in the public realm if not to effect a particular outcome?" Arendt reminds us of the fact that participation in public is the way to be seen: through acting in public we "disclose" our identity. In other words, in the process of sharing our perspectives in the public realm, and being seen and judged by others, people tell stories about who they and others are. These stories, Arendt suggests, capture our identity: not "what" we are as in our gender or ethnicity, but "who" we are as in what perspectives on the world we hold. These are the stories and actions through which our identities are disclosed and they "reveal an agent, but this agent is not an author or producer."[9] To say that the speaking subject is an agent who is neither the author nor the producer of his or her own story is to recognize that individuals often have little control over how their utterances are understood or what they come to mean to others. We may articulate a claim or act in a way that is meant to convey identity, but our intentions and our understanding are not the determining factors in the meaning given to our utterances and actions given that such utterances take place in a realm populated by individuals with different and partial perspectives. Members of political communities will interpret our utterances in a variety of ways; they will tell multiple and perhaps contradictory stories about our actions likely to have little to do with what we had intended. We should embrace this contingency, Arendt suggests, because its rests on a commitment to human plurality and judgment, as well as evinces a recognition of human freedom and a faith in the possibility of the new. *Peithein*, in other words, is a practice of freedom, whether of thought, of action, of shifting perspective, that makes the new or unexpected possible:

> This freedom of movement, then—whether as the freedom to depart and begin something new and unheard-of or as the freedom to interact in speech with many others and experience the diversity that the world always is in its totality—most certainly was and is not the end purpose of politics, that is, something that can be achieved by political means. It is rather the substance and meaning of all things political.[10]

Embracing a particularly perlocutionary understanding of persuasion (e.g., one in which uncertainty of outcome is expected) as an essential political practice is, of course, considerably at odds with the dominant Western understanding of politics. Indeed, according to Arendt, since the days of Plato, philosophers have sought to subordinate the realm of human affairs to the realm of philosophy, to contain a world of contingency and uncertainty through the application of philosophical rules. But this is, according to Arendt, actually "an escape from politics altogether."[11] In giving pride of place to the application of philosophical reasoning to the realm of human affairs, in casting aside a politics of persuasive claims-making, in embracing a means-ends understanding of politics, we—thanks in large part to Plato—obscure the fact that "[p]olitics deals with the coexistence and association of *different* men" who have various opinions or perspectives on the world that are not necessarily shared by or agreeable to all.[12] This disregards and degrades the distinctly human activity of sharing perspectives and ultimately robs the world of new ways of seeing and interacting. From Arendt's perspective, this insistence on being able to determine the philosophical principles by which one can rightly organize political life continues to dominate the political thinking of the Western world, at great cost to ourselves. Lost in the desire to find the universal truths and abstract rules with which to determine the course of public interaction are the very activities and opportunities that make us human. Lost is the willingness and courage to share individual opinions and perspectives, to disagree and debate, and to make judgments—all of which are activities essential to human freedom and captured in the practice of persuasion.

That Arendt is championing a politics of persuasion does not necessarily mean, however, that she champions a politics of rights claiming.
Indeed, on some interpretations of her work, Arendt's understanding of
politics explicity rejects rights claiming—or at least the claiming of
human rights. Her writings, particularly on the rights claiming of stateless persons before and during World War II, seem to suggest as much.
When rights claims were made by individuals without nation-state citizenship status, she reminds us, they proved to be quite a disaster. Claims
made by stateless persons and in the face of the horrific abuses of to-
talitarian regimes went unheeded and failed to protect individuals from
grave harm. Their meaningfulness and power proved to be tied up with
precisely the membership in a nation-state that the rights claimants
lacked. Persons rendered stateless were basically rendered rightless:
when individuals had only those rights that were supposed to exist
beyond the state to fall back on for protection and recognition, they
found that there was "no authority . . . left to protect [these rights] and no
institution . . . willing to guarantee them."[13] If rights claiming was meant
to change the situation of the stateless, Arendt seems to suggest, the
practice failed and failed, in part, because of a faulty understanding of
the nature of rights themselves: they are not the irrefutable birthrights
of human beings. That Arendt reveals rights claims to be anything but
trumping claims with indisputable metaphysical foundations has led
some scholars to read her as contributing to arguments outlining the
philosophical bankruptcy of rights theory and the political impotence of
rights claiming.[14] I would argue, however, that Arendt's discussion of
the rights claims of the stateless actually sheds light on the perlocutionary nature and democratic character of the utterances. Rights claims, she
shows us, never trump because of their particular philosophical definition and we cannot guarantee the efficacy of the claim by adopting a set
of rules in advance. Instead, rights claims are revealed to be equivocal
utterances that are made in the context of a public composed of a plurality of perspectives and thus open to differing interpretations.

That rights claims are characterized by radical contingency need not be
reason for despair or for rejection of rights altogether. Certainly not if we
place rights claiming in the context of a politics of *peithein* and thus recognize rights as perspectival claims rather than absolute truths. From this
perspective, the lesson of supposed rights failure is not that we should no
longer challenge indignity through recourse to rights language but, rather,
that we must recognize that rights claiming is not enough. It is not enough

to make rights claims and expect that they command assent because they describe some irrefutable fact about the world or human nature or because we have followed a set of rules precisely. Instead, we must recognize that the very meaning and power of the rights claims are agreed upon and given reality by communities of individuals. They are not discovered nor given by human nature but, rather, created through the process of civic engagement, debate, and deliberation; and they, therefore, require that citizens "act in concert" to constitute their meaning and ensure their preservation and power. Rights do not, and cannot, as the experiences of totalitarianism teach, exist independent of and prior to politics. Nor are rights protected and preserved through a constitution, a bill of rights, or even a democratic state alone. Indeed, it is the political activity of citizens that gives rights claims their meaning and power. The right to engage in political activity, the right and space to share opinions and act in concert with others—these are, for Arendt, more fundamental and essential to human well-being and freedom than even the rights of citizens, and such rights are only guaranteed by those who actively claim them.

I am suggesting, then, that we place Arendt's discussion of rights claiming in the context of her embrace of a Socratic understanding of politics. This entails adopting an understanding of the practice of rights claiming that eschews precisely the expectations that are implicit in a rights-as-trumps conception. To accept that politics is about sharing opinions and making claims of persuasion rather than necessarily persuading another, proposing absolute truths that can compel assent, or even fixing the rules in advance to guarantee specific outcomes, the political actor must forgo the expectation that he or she can control the outcome of political claims making. This requires that rights-claiming individuals embrace a politics of uncertainty rather than the politics of instrumentality and means-ends calculations that we often associate with the rights-as-trumps metaphor. Making rights claims, on this account, means recognizing that however forcefully one may assert her claim or however much she believes her perspective to be right or true, she must accept that it is still a perspectival claim rather than an absolute truth, a perlocutionary utterance rather than an illocutionary utterance, a perspective rather than a trump. Moreover, she must accept that because rights claims are expressions of individual ways of seeing the world, and because they are made in the context of a plurality of perspectives, their acceptance is something over which we have little control, their felicity never assured. On this account, rights claims are more akin to aesthetic claims than to mathematical formulas or absolute truths, and thus open to disagreement. As Linda Zerilli reminds us, just as we can never force another to agree that a painting is beautiful, "there is no single argument that can or should persuade everyone capable of reason, regardless of standpoint or context, of a particular . . . political judgment."[15] Likewise, we can never force another to agree that I or we have a right to something. That is a conclusion that results from the judgment of the listener and not an effect that can be guaranteed by the intention behind a speaker's words, the words she chooses, or even the circumstances under which she speaks. Rights claiming is a perlocutionary activity that entails the sharing of different, multiple, and often divergent and conflicting points of view, and is thus always open to the interpretation and judgment of others.[16]

Though there is debate about Arendt's reading of Greek history, as well as her arguments about rights, what I want to emphasize here is the value she places on engaging with others and on the importance of embracing the unpredictability of that engagement. Both of these, I am suggesting, have important implications for understanding the practice of making rights claims. Speaking and acting in public, such as we do when we make rights claims, requires that we recognize that each individual has a unique perspective on the world. To share our perspectives with others, and to welcome theirs in turn, requires openness to seeing the world from a variety of perspectives beyond our own. Moreover, it requires acknowledging that we cannot guarantee outcomes no matter how much we would like to. Rights claims, on this understanding, are not trumps because they are not irresistible and irrefutable claims that promise particular results; they are, instead, claims of persuasion. Rights claiming is, then, an activity that involves presenting, debating, and contesting opinions or perspectives. It requires recognizing the plurality of opinions and individuals and embracing the fact that what we do in the political realm entails a great degree of risk and a willingness to accept that one can never guarantee a particular outcome.[17]

This does not mean, however, that rights claiming or any practice of persuasion precludes the possibility of making judgments or even coming to agreement. Opinions, Arendt reminds us, are not mere "subjective fantasy" or wholly arbitrary points of view. Coming to agreement, achieving some kind of objectivity, is possible, though not as we might assume. "'[O]bjectivity,'" Arendt explains, "resides in the fact that the same world opens up to everyone and that despite all the differences between men and their positions in the world—and consequently their *doxai* (opinions)—'both you and I are human.'"[18] What makes a claim persuasive is not the fact that it exists in some realm beyond the world of human affairs but, rather, what it makes visible. As Zerilli explains, "If an argument has 'force,' it is more as a vehicle of imaginative 'seeing' . . . than an irrefutable logic."[19] The point here is that the meaning and outcome of our utterance is not reducible either to an absolute, objective truth or to our most sincere intentions. It is, instead, constituted in the context of a plurality of perspectives. Making claims of persuasion in the public realm, in other words, involves asking of ourselves and others that we consider the point of view—the ideas, beliefs, and commitments—of our fellow citizens. As Garsten argues, persuasion is important for democratic politics because it "draws us out of ourselves"— that is, it "require[s] us to step outside our particular perspectives without asking us to leave our particular commitments behind."[20] Agreements are thus reached only through sharing perspectives on the world with others and seeing the world through their eyes, but such agreements must then be recognized and embraced as contingent and always open to reinterpretation and contestation.

Below I offer more concrete examples of what it means to understand the performativity of rights claiming in terms of the activity of persuasion. To do this, I turn to the work of John Stuart Mill, a theorist usually read as a quintessential liberal thinker whose work provides an early defense of the rights-as-trumps metaphor. Against this interpretation, I argue that Mill actually advances an understanding of rights claiming as a practice of persuasion. Moreover, in his own political practice, he sheds light on the fact that the value of rights claiming lies in its ability not necessarily to constrain the actions of governments or individuals but, rather, to provide opportunities for individuals to practice being democratic citizens.

Who Makes Rights Claims? Rereading Mill on Rights

John Stuart Mill's work has been described as expressing the fundamental commitments of liberal political theory, as representing the very heart of liberalism. Given its embrace and promotion of a strong commitment to individual freedom and its seemingly individualistic conception of the rights-bearing subject, Mill's writings are traditionally read as promoting a conception of rights-as-trumps that is not only counter-majoritarian, but also at odds with the values needed to make democracy flourish.[21] This reading is not without grounds. Mill certainly does tell us that with regard to action that "merely concerns himself," an individual's "independence is, of right, absolute" and that "Over himself, over his own body and mind, the individual is sovereign."[22] It would seem that Mill embraces what Charles Taylor calls the primacy of rights and atomism theses because of his very explicit commitment to seeing individuals as the best judges of their own interest and his argument that individual and social development are more likely to be enhanced by leaving individuals to themselves than by their being influenced by impulsive majorities.[23] Rights, Mill seems to suggest, are precisely what protect individuals from the pernicious influence of social forces: "To have rights is to have something which society ought to defend me in the possession of" not because, as natural rights scholars and social contract thinkers suggest, rights adhere to individuals by virtue of their humanity or because they are the natural birthright of human beings, but because they allow for human development.[24] Indeed, to make a rights claim appears to be, for Mill, to put down the ultimate trump card. When individuals claim rights that allow them to protect their own freedom without doing harm to others the *ought* and *should* implicit in the rights claim "grow into *must.*"[25] If, however, we consider Mill's arguments in light of some of his political activities and from the perspective of the theory of performativity developed in the preceding pages, a different understanding emerges. Mill should be read, I argue, as advocating a politics of persuasion in which the practice of rights claiming is a perspectival rather than a trumping activity. Rights claiming, on this account, is a valuable practice for democratic societies not because it results in specific policy or legal ends but because it provides opportunities for civic engagement and the cultivation of political judgment. Such a counterintuitive reading of Mill's defense of individual liberty and understanding of rights rests on a very particular interpretation of his theory of the subject and thus I begin here.

It is in Mill's *System of Logic (The Logic)* that we find him working through what it means for individuals to be free and where we find that this freedom is not characterized by a radical separation from others. In this work, particularly the chapter "Of Liberty and Necessity," we see Mill's frustration with the metaphysical distinctions between freedom and determinism that he has inherited and find him struggling to articulate a theory of human subjectivity that avoids the extremes of both the doctrines of free will and of necessity popular during his day. It is here that we get a glimpse of his deep investment in the kind of intersubjective dimensions of human character that his critics find missing in his work. For Mill, who we are, what we do, how we think—our volitions and our actions—are not the result of being left alone, nor do individuals flourish that way, isolated in their sphere of freedom, protected from social forces by a set of inviolable borders. In fact, it is almost impossible, Mill suggests, to conceive of individuals as isolatable from social forces or to imagine character as emanating from some pure form of unshaped consciousness or will. As he explains in *The Subjection of Women*, it would be impossible to "isolate a human being from the circumstances of his condition, so as to ascertain experimentally what he would have been by nature."[26] All that we can do is consider the individual in his or her context, as affected by various—perhaps even limitless—influences and forces.

Mill's recognition of the social locatedness and relationality of individuals is rooted in his embrace and modification of what was called, at the time, the doctrine of necessity. The doctrine of necessity posited that human actions had identifiable causes. It showed that "our volitions and actions are invariable consequents of our antecedent states of mind."[27] From Mill's perspective, this meant that human behavior had to be attributed to causal factors in much the same way that movement in the physical world would be attributed to physical causes. For example our education, our upbringing, our work experiences—all these would shape our character and inform our temperament and our actions. What was taken to be natural about men or women, for example, female modesty or male aggressiveness, would have to be understood as the product of our educational, social, familial, and political environments. If these circumstances were to change, our characters would change and this, in turn, would change the decisions we would make and the actions we would take.

Such an attribution of human behavior to causal laws and external influences was quite alarming to many. Proponents of the doctrine of free will balked at the idea that human volitions were the effects of external influences and thought that such a belief was "inconsistent with every one's instinctive consciousness, as well as humiliating to the pride and even degrading to the moral nature of man."[28] If all of human behavior were attributable to a specific cause, how could we explain our feelings of free will, and what kind of responsibility or accountability would be left for the individual? We would all be social dupes. Mill, however, believed otherwise. His particular understanding of the doctrine of necessity explicitly rejected the idea that individuals were socially determined. Indeed, he argued that causation was actually consistent, rather than inconsistent, with much of our experience. Empirically, our experiences were more likely to confirm than to dumbfound causal explanations of our actions. Philosophically, causation had never been completely at odds with doctrines of free will. One needed just consider religious doctrines to realize that freedom of the will could be consistent with antecedent causes such as God's will. To be free, in other words, need not foreclose the possibility that our actions have antecedent causes, empirically or philosophically. In fact, to believe otherwise, Mill suggested, was to make a potentially grave error, and to embrace a "false philosophy." For Mill, the doctrine of free will divorced from any theory of causation was not only incorrect but also dangerous: "The notion that truths external to the mind may be known by intuition or consciousness, independently of observation and experience, is, I am persuaded, in these times, the great intellectual support of false doctrines and bad institutions."[29]

In rejecting the doctrine of free will, Mill was careful to distinguish himself from those who adopted a stricter interpretation of the doctrine of necessity and assumed an absolute determinism to human behavior. Proponents of the strict interpretation, he argued, make as grave an error as proponents of the doctrine of free will when they posit an irresistibility or absolute determinism to human actions. Simply "[b]ecause something will certainly happen if nothing is done to prevent it," does not mean that "it will certainly happen whatever may be done to prevent it."[30] Given that there is no "mysterious compulsion" that determines the shape of our all actions, Mill suggested replacing the term "necessity" with the term "causation." "The application of so improper a term as Necessity to the doctrine of cause and effect in the matter of human character seems to me one of the most signal instances in philosophy of abuse of terms. . . . The subject will never be generally understood, until that objectionable term is dropped."[31] Mill's modified doctrine of necessity or causation draws attention not to what *must* happen but only to what *may* happen, given certain circumstances. Certain things will occur if unimpeded. For example, while it may be true that we will die if we go without food or air, it need not be inevitable that the lack of food or air will lead to our death. Causation did not, according to Mill, entail a *must*, for there were many other factors that would come into play to alter the outcome of particular causes: "human actions are . . . never . . . ruled by any one motive with such absolute sway, that there is no room for the influenced of another."[32] Moreover, it would not be possible to know all the circumstances that influence action and volition. So numerous and varied are the circumstances that shape an individual's character that it would be difficult, if not impossible, to determine precisely which influences caused which effects. These facts rendered the doctrine of necessity far less absolute and determinist, far more unpredictable and contingent, than some thought.[33]

Mill's rejection of the strict interpretation of the doctrine of necessity was premised on more than simply an awareness of the potentially infinite circumstances that may shape a person's character. He also recognized something that is beyond the reach of circumstances and is, in fact, to be considered a circumstance itself. One of those innumerable circumstances that shapes individual character and generates diversity of character and unpredictability of action is our feeling of moral power, the "power to alter [our] character." While refusing to call this free will, Mill described it as a "feeling of our being able to modify our own character *if we wish*," and he remained committed to seeing this power as consistent with the modified doctrine of necessity he embraced. He saw it as a perversion of the doctrine of necessity to believe that one's "character is formed *for* him, not *by* him" for "[w]e are exactly as capable of making our own character, *if we will*, as others are of making it for us."[34] As Mill explained elsewhere, this power to modify our character derives, in part, from the fact that individuals are born with certain capacities that include the ability to use their minds and senses to perceive the world around them. Individuals have the ability to make distinctions and discriminate among competing ideas and desires, to make judgments and to register preferences. These capacities are both rational and sentimental. They include an ability to make sense of the world not only through logic but also through feelings, particularly the feelings of sympathy and self-defense that actually connect us with others.[35] When we recognize the many ways in which circumstances can interact to encourage or curtail these capacities and instincts, it becomes clear that human beings have potentially limitless possibilities. In fact, it is only in social context and through social relations, through the "artificial discipline" of education, legislation, and social arrangements, that these potentials and capacities come to have meaning.

For Mill, unraveling the mystery of human subjectivity required rejecting facile depictions of individuals as either purely free-willing and self-interested or as unwitting social dupes. Recognizing an element of truth contained in both the doctrine of necessity and the doctrine of free will, Mill suggested that the two be joined together in order to more accurately and adequately capture the human experience. Human beings must be understood as simultaneously influenced by and yet capable of modifying the linguistic and social communities in which they are embedded, as actively engaged in making sense of the world around them and in practices of persuasion and judgment. It is in Mill's understanding of rights claiming, as well as his own engagement in rights politics, that these capacities and practices are illuminated.

Why Make Rights Claims?

What bearing does Mill's ontology have on his understanding of the practice of rights claiming? What is being done when someone makes a rights claim if there is no sovereign subject trying to set boundaries between him or herself and others? When we take seriously Mill's recognition of the social dimensions of subjectivity, it becomes clear that he did not, as traditional readings would have it, imagine that individuals deployed rights claims in order to isolate themselves from all other social influences. In fact, his appreciation of the fact that individuals do not, or even cannot, develop best when left completely alone informs Mill's defense of rights claiming as a site of the practice of persuasion and the exercise of judgment. In making rights claims, that is, individuals learn to share their perspectives on the world with others while considering the views and feelings of those with whom they share a community, and they do this in ways that draw on both reason and sentient. In the process, they create and reshape the boundaries and meanings of individual identity and community. Consider Mill's arguments about rights in *Utilitarianism*. Though we usually read Mill's description of rights in terms of absolutism and divisiveness, Mill actually offers a challenge to the rights-as-trumps conception. As Mill explains, a right, or rather "the idea of *a right*," represents a particular set of feelings, beliefs, and demands that we commonly associate with justice. The idea of a right brings together both our *ideas* of justice—what we understand intellectually or what Mill associates with our rational instincts—and our *sentiments* of justice, or what we feel or what Mill associates with the animal instincts. A rights claim, he is suggesting, is not simply the instrument, that is, tool we bring out at a particular time in the game of politics. Instead, it is an activity through which we try to capture and express our reason and our feelings, our understanding of the rules that determine injury or violation, as well as our desire for retaliation and revenge. Rights claiming expresses a hurt and enacts a demand, or at least a provisional one, based on a perception of a violation or injury and a common desire to punish or retaliate. This knowledge and these feelings, Mill explains, have roots in the complex and powerful mix of self-interest and connectedness, of concern with defending the self and sympathy toward others, as well as recognition that we are embedded in communities with existing norms and conventions.

Mill presents us with a picture of the practice of rights claiming as one that involves both our reasons and our sentiments. When we call something a right, when we speak of violations of rights, we mean that there has been some violation of a rule of conduct, some injury, and we demand punishment out of a desire for revenge.[36] When we make rights claims not only are we sharing our own feelings and reasons with others but we are also attempting to see the world from their point of view. As Mill explains, the desire for retaliation that motivates a rights claim is an intense feeling shared by all sentient beings rooted in a common need for security. And this feeling gives a rights claim the sense of absoluteness. That, however, does not make a rights claim a moral claim. As Mill explains in *Utilitarianism*, absoluteness is associated with an animal feeling manifest in a desire for retaliation rather than being based in anything purely rational or intellectual. A rights claim becomes a moral claim only when this desire is combined with what he calls "superior intelligence" or "enlarged sympathy." The sentiment of justice that stems from a desire for revenge only becomes moral when it is subordinated to "the social sympathies." Rights claims must consider the interests of society as a whole and recognize the individual as a part of that society in order to be moral; otherwise, they are simply the expression of sentiments untempered by social feelings. In other words, justice and morality, often manifest in rights claims, do not derive from purely individualistic desires for revenge. Such desires must be subordinated to social feeling and it is enlarged sympathy that moves us from an individualistic thirst for retaliation back into the community where thought, discussion, and debate are central. It is in the process of claiming rights, then, that individuals have an opportunity to engage in the very practices central to the creation and cultivation of democratic citizens and communities. This practice provides individuals with an opportunity to consult their reason as well as their feelings, giving due weight to both in light of their membership in a larger community. It allows—indeed, requires—individuals to consider the world not only from their own perspective but from the perspectives of others as well.

Rights claiming thus offers an apt example of the intersubjective activities that Mill champions throughout his work. Contrary to the more

traditional readings of Mill as an anti-democratic elitist, as wholly concerned with protecting atomistic individuals from the influences of the
state and society, Mill's work as a whole, and his defense of the rights such
as freedom of thought and expression, are better read in light of his
embrace of participation in public life.[37] Freedoms, often manifest in particular legal rights, are important to Mill because they offer opportunities
for the development of the individual capacities for perception and judgment, as well as the development of affective ties between individuals and
a sense of care for the community.[38] Human beings, Mill reminds us, are
fallible, prone to make serious errors in judgment that are then codified in
legislation and action. These errors are only corrected through debate,
deliberation, and contestation of ideas and opinions. But freedom of
thought and expression are valuable not simply because they may allow us
to replace falsehood with truth or to develop new ideas and displace pernicious ones, but also, and perhaps more important, because it is through
contestation and engagement with differences of perspective that one
comes to be fully human. "Judgment," Mill argues, "is given to men that
they may use it."[39] Like any other muscle, it must be exercised in order for
it to remain strong, and it can be exercised through lively discussion that
forces us to examine our deeply held beliefs. Thus, it is through acting on
our opinions and challenging presumed social truths, acting and speaking
in public, that we exercise and improve the very faculties that make us
human. And for Mill, it is best to do this in ways that are contestatory.

As Jeremy Waldron argues, Mill greatly appreciates the value of "moral
distress" or "ethical confrontation." Differences of opinion and variation among lifestyles often come into conflict, and this "open clash between
earnestly-held ideals and opinions about the nature and basis of the good
life" is essential to individual and social progress.[40] In Mill's words, debate
and discussion require the "reconciling and combining opposites" that is
"a rough process of a struggle between combatants fighting under hostile
banners."[41] And though having one's fundamental beliefs and practices
questioned may be painful, individuals develop open-mindedness, a tol-
erance of difference, and the ability to listen as well as persuade in the
process. For Mill, then, antagonism between individuals and groups
holding different opinions is not rooted in an innate competitiveness or a
desire for isolation and absolute separation. Rather, politics as a process of
refutation and contestation is a result of the deficiencies of the human
mind and the usefulness of such challenges. In politics, Mill explains,
opposition is healthy: "it is almost commonplace, that a party of order or

stability, and a party of progress or reform, are both necessary elements of a healthy state of political life."[42]

In fact, Mill explicitly denounces the idea of a "frictionless" society. "Without the right to protest, and the capacity for it, there is . . . no justice, there are no ends worth pursuing."[43] The right to protest prevents error and even truth from "hardening into prejudice" and helps to prevent the development of passive individuals who lack the courage to think and act in new and different ways. Passivity or "peace in the intellectual world" is not, Mill writes in *On Liberty*, desirable if it means conformity of opinion and action. "[T]he price paid for this sort of intellectual pacification, is the sacrifice of the entire moral courage of the human mind." Without lively debates over social norms and customs, society will not generate "the open, fearless characters, and logical, consistent intellects who once adorned the world." But this character is not reserved for the geniuses or the elite. As if anticipating charges of elitism, Mill argues that freedom of thought is as important to the individual of average intellect as it is to the great thinkers. In fact, it is "even more indispensable, to enable average human beings to attain the mental stature which they are capable of." A few great minds may be able to survive in a society in which there is despotism and uniformity of opinion, but "an intellectually active people" will never be produced under conditions of "mental slavery."[44]

This is not to deny that Mill is concerned about the tenor of public debate and deliberation. He does argue for temperance and respectful disagreement. "The free expression of all opinions," Mill suggests, "should be permitted, on condition that the manner be temperate, and do not pass the bounds of fair discussion."[45] "Vituperative language" and other unsavory tactics that might stifle certain opinions must also be rejected. However, Mill denounces a disorderly politics not because he desires harmony or unemotional debates but, rather, because he is concerned that tactics of bullying and denouncing opponents get used to silence certain ideas, particularly those that challenge and refute social norms and customs. The argument for temperance is not an argument for temperance as a good in and of itself but, rather, as a tool meant to safeguard the space for different voices and perspectives, to allow outrage and divergent opinions a place in politics, and to make space for that one voice, that one person with a contrary opinion at risk of being muted. Indeed, what we see Mill doing here is defending a particular kind of persuasive speaking, one that differs from manipulation or coercion to the extent that it respects the capacity of its listeners to make judgments.[46]

Mill's robust defense of individual liberty, one of the most often claimed rights, is not an attack on social relations in total but, rather, an attack on those relations that shut down ethical confrontation. Uncontested acceptance of public opinion and a lack of opportunities for political participation undermine the general well-being of individuals and society. As Mill suggests, a society that willingly accepts the opinions of a few without contestation or critical engagement becomes a society of "sheep" who simply follow rules and a society without strong affective ties. In fact, communal ties are produced through social activities such as the participation in social and political life. In *Considerations on Representative Government*, for example, Mill argues that individuals who are denied the right to vote in elections or a voice in the governance of a society become indifferent to social well-being and learn not to care about what happens to others. Under a despotic government, the mental faculties of human beings are deprived of exercise and thereby "stunted," and social connections are disbanded. "Whenever the sphere of action of human beings is artificially circumscribed," Mill argues, "their sentiments are narrowed and dwarfed in the same proportion. . . . Let a person have nothing to do for his country, and he will not care for it."[47]

My point here is that Mill's understanding of rights reiterates the themes of a politics of persuasion. With its emphasis on sharing one's perspective on the world with others and being open to seeing it from their perspectives as well, with its embrace of perspectives constituted by reason and feeling, and with its acceptance of the fact that intentions do not guarantee particular political outcomes, Millian rights claiming, like a number of his other examples of public engagement, are important sites of and for the practice of judgment. As Nadia Urbinati points out, Mill's emphasis on deliberation and participation takes its inspiration from the Athens of Socrates rather than Plato, and thus it places a high value on the capacities of citizens to form opinions and make judgments. But such capacities must be continually exercised for them not to atrophy, and this requires activities such as rights claiming that provide the forum to instill in citizens a "sense of mutuality and unity."[48]

Being Persuasive

Mill's interest in creating spaces for and supporting the activities of persuasion and judgment was not just theoretical. Indeed, his own engagement in politics exemplifies the kind of deliberative practices and

rights-claiming activities I am suggesting he championed in his philosophical works. Consider Mill's work on behalf of women's rights. Mill's
defense of women's rights begins from recognizing the concerns and perspectives of his contemporaries. Rather than simply rejecting the idea
that women are uninterested in and perhaps even unfit for politics and
business, Mill offers an alternative explanation for the facts of "women's
character." Poor character, he explains, is not naturally determined by
women's biology but is, rather, the result of external circumstances,
"forced repression in some directions, unnatural stimulation in others."
Good character, he continues, would thus develop in women when they
were free to pursue their own paths in life.[49] Let women have the same
rights and freedoms as men, Mill continues, and they will blossom in
ways that are good for men and children as well. In presenting his perspective on women's rights and character, Mill takes seriously the concerns and fears of his interlocutors. And while he offers a set of reasons
to justify women's liberty, he also engages the sentiments of his audience.
Indeed, it is precisely his engagement with the fears of men reflected in
his statements that women, when given the choice, will nonetheless
remain caretakers of the house and family that is criticized for weakening,
if not wholly undermining, the feminist impact of his arguments. What
is often read as a reflection of Mill's deep-seated Victorian paternalism
can, I am suggesting, be read as part of the practice of persuasion, a practice that requires engaging others where they are as one tries to move
them to embrace an alternative perspective.

Perhaps an even more apt illustration of rights claiming as a practice
of persuasion comes from Mill's engagement in the debate over the Contagious Diseases Acts (CD Acts). In 1864, the British Parliament responded
to the spread of venereal disease among military personnel by calling for
an elaborate system for the surveillance and regulation of female prostitutes. The CD Acts, reauthorized in 1866 and 1869, presumed women to
be the source of infection and, therefore, the proper targets of arrest, detainment, and forced medical examination. Women suspected of being
prostitutes were arrested and asked to submit to examination. If a woman
refused, she was brought before a magistrate who would then determine
whether she was, in fact, a prostitute and was therefore required to undergo examination. If found to be infected, she was then interned in a
Lock hospital for up to six months, until she received a clean bill of health.

When the Acts were about to be reauthorized in 1869, and the reach
of police powers to watch and arrest extended beyond discrete military

districts, a large repeal effort began. Mill was an active and vocal member of this campaign. From his perspective, there was no doubt that the Acts clearly violated women's right to privacy and individual liberty, and expanded the power of the state in directions both unnecessary and dangerous. To make this point, Mill offered challenging testimony that drew upon a wide variety of moral, legal, and political arguments meant to address not just the reasons behind the Acts but also the fears and passions motivating it. Mill's testimony is, then, an apt illustration of a politics of persuasion, a deliberative activity in which one advances particular perspectives on an issue while acknowledging the perspectives of others and accepting the indeterminacy of outcomes. What we see is Mill engaging in what Garsten, drawing on Aristotle, calls the exercise of "situated judgment," "a more or less continuous activity of both constructing and dismantling standards, holding one commitment provisionally steady while evaluating others in light of it."[50]

Among the standards Mill found most disconcerting and in need of dismantling were those having to do with notions of male and female sexuality. Supporters of the Acts justified the regulation of prostitutes with the argument that men had naturally uncontrollable sexual urges and therefore needed safe outlets for their sexual desires while women did not. Women, according to this interpretation, were not only able but also expected to control their sexual impulses, while the men were presumed to be beyond control. Indeed, Mill makes the case for women's right to freedom from the prying eyes of the state by challenging the fundamental presuppositions of the Acts themselves. According to Mill, the Acts were not simply at odds with a growing social commitment to individual liberty but also they reinforced some unfortunate notions about male sexual desire. To believe that men needed a safe outlet for their sexual urges, and that these outlets were best protected through the arrest and detainment of suspected prostitutes, was something Mill found absurd. Such presuppositions failed, from Mill's perspective, to appreciate the processes of causation, overestimating the "naturalness" of both female degradation and masculine sexual urges. Illicit male sexuality, he argued, was actually promoted, if not produced, by the Acts themselves. By providing men with a safe outlet for their sexual urges, the CD Acts fostered men's sexual transgressions, leaving "the impression on the minds of soldiers and sailors . . . that it is not discouraged, that it is considered by Parliament a necessity which may be regulated, but which must be accepted, and that Parliament does not entertain any serious disapprobation of immoral conduct of that kind."[51] In making "illicit indulgence" safe, Parliament cultivated the very unruly male sexuality it presumed to be so natural. And this, from Mill's perspective, was a wretched arrangement that needed to be rectified, not through increasing men's freedom but through curtailing it. To address the problem of troop readiness by making illicit sex safe for men was to "pander to [men's] vices" and to create such a system was to offer "a monstrous artificial cure for a monstrous artificial evil which had far better be swept away at its root in accordance with democratic principles of government."[52]

In keeping with his commitment to the doctrine of necessity and his recognition of the intersubjective and causal dimensions of subjectivity, Mill also suggested that public education about the threat of disease transmission or laws criminalizing disease transmission to wives be enacted. Such policies would encourage men to change their behavior, cultivating their ability to control their sexual desires. Persuasion, advice, and information could and would, in his opinion, lead to important behavior changes. For Mill, there was nothing naturally uncontrollable about male sexuality. Rather, like women's supposedly natural inferiority or female prostitutes' supposedly natural pathology, men's supposed sexual propensity was actually a product of the very social arrangements presumed to reflect it. In challenging dominant conceptions of male sexuality, Mill also challenged the dominant Victorian conceptions of female sexuality. The double standard allowed and accepted male sexual license while it expected purity and virtue from women. Evidence of female sexual license (i.e., prostitution) was thus taken as evidence of the loss of femininity or womanhood defined in terms of purity and virtue. This interpretation of the female body led to a rather odd and somewhat contradictory position on prostitution. On the one hand, supporters argued that the women who were engaged in prostitution had lost all traces of their femininity or womanhood and were therefore already so degraded that surveillance and examination could not degrade them further. On the other hand, supporters justified the regulation with the argument that such legislation would eventually lead to the reclamation of these women, thereby assuming there was some femininity left to be salvaged. These arguments were further complicated by supporters' refusal to allow the examination of men. Whereas examination of prostitutes was not seen as degrading, examination of men was. These arguments were not entirely convincing to Mill. While he agreed with supporters that female sexuality could be controlled, that it was not naturally unruly, he also believed that men could control their sexuality. And although he agreed that men could be degraded by the examination, he believed that they would be much less degraded than most women: "Men are not lowered in their own eyes as much by exposure of their persons."[53] Mill thus made claims for women's rights by exposing and disputing the dominant conceptions of male sexuality and the sexual double standard implicit in the Acts. By calling attention to the inequality perpetrated by the legislation, Mill not only challenged Parliament to rethink its public health policy but also challenged his society to rethink dominant conceptions of male and female sexuality.

To be sure, Mill's defense of women's rights, like his defense of rights in general, has its problems. While he defends women's rights and contests dominant conceptions of female inferiority by describing "character" or identity as something that is artificially and socially constituted, Mill also uses essentialized notions of gender identity to achieve the same purposes. This shift between a recognition of the mutability of identity and the naturalization of character leads Mill not only to argue for women's freedom from state interference but also to support a host of state- and socially-based disciplinary practices that are quite worrisome.[54] But it is his understanding of the very porousness of the subject, not a belief in impermeable boundaries and inviolable egos, and his efforts to recognize the concerns of his audience, that leads Mill to champion individual freedom at the same time that he champions both participation in politics and the intervention of the state. If we appreciate the extent to which Mill embraced a modified doctrine of necessity, the extent to which he believed individual character to be the product of artificial cultivation, then we can understand better why he would support some invasive public policies and not others. For example, Mill suggested that military men be watched and examined in order to reduce the likelihood of their transmitting disease to their wives. He also suggested that a law be made to penalize men who were found guilty of such transmission, subjecting them to monetary penalties and allowing their wives the right to divorce them. Such policies, he believed, would have the potential to discourage men from soliciting prostitutes and thereby reduce the threat of venereal disease.

One could say that he supports these policies because they address a clear harm—the transmission of venereal disease. However, the possibility of harm is not enough to explain why Mill supports intervention into men's lives and yet demands that women be free from state interference. Moreover, harm is always a necessary but not sufficient condition to justify intervention into the lives of others. What is important in my reading of Mill is not that he seeks to protect individuals against any and all forms of majoritarian tyranny but, rather, that he seeks to cultivate character in specific ways that enable the development of the capacities for perception and judgment. In fact, one could even read Mill's defense of women's privacy rights as an effort, not to set up a sphere of unfettered freedom, but to cultivate women's character as well. Improvements in women's morality and health, Mill argued, would be more likely to result from their having the freedom to make health-care decisions for themselves than from their being forced to undergo medical examination and treatment. Arrest, detainment, and forced medical treatment would only degrade women's character, while "the mere existence of hospitals" and care provided by "benevolent and excellent people" would help turn women from a life of prostitution to one of moral propriety.[55] Mill's defense of women's liberty, of their right to privacy and freedom from state intervention, while seemingly able to provide a space for women's flourishing, upon closer examination appears to be intended to improve their character by urging their relocation to different webs of social relations, not abstracting them from these relations altogether.[56]

There are, of course, dangers in making an argument for rights based on the recognition of intersubjectivity and the fears of your audience—perils that result from linking rights to the cultivation of character. These include a tendency to transform rights into a moral discourse that seeks to distinguish those fit for rights-bearing subjectivity from those unfit for it, and to punish or constrain those deemed unfit. This is certainly a concern raised by some contemporary readings of Mill's work, and it is an issue I address in greater detail in later chapters.[57] But what is important for my argument is to turn attention elsewhere, to shed light on the fact that Millian rights claiming is part of an active, participatory ethos that helps to constitute community and provides the space for the contestation of the arrangements and identity categories constitutive of that very community. Though Mill clearly evinces an anxiety about the detrimental effects that social relations may have on human character, his understanding of what enables human development and how rights can function are, nonetheless, far more complicated than traditional readings of Mill as a liberal individualist would suggest. Human beings do not, he teaches, develop their human capacities in isolation but, rather, through engagement with other individuals. And rights claims are an essential element of that participation. Not only do rights claims reflect the socially situated qualities of individuals, as they reflect the partiality and plurality of perspectives, but it is also through the practice of rights claiming, through rights-based political activity, that individual identity is contested and reconstituted and that communities are formed. With John Stuart Mill, then, we learn that instability and mutability at the level of identity, while anxiety producing, can also be a source of democratic political promise.

Reading Mill as advancing an understanding of rights as claims of persuasion—as perspectival claims that also acknowledge the perspectives of others and their capacities to make judgments—helps us recognize that this practice actually allows for the contestation and creation, rather than simply the solidification, of different understandings of individual subjectivity and democratic community. It also reminds us that rights themselves are not things we have that are independent of our relationships with others, but are instead the product of contestation and practices of intersubjective meaning making. Their very meaning and power are not discovered philosophically nor given by human nature but are, instead, created through the process of civic engagement, debate, and deliberation. Moreover, understanding rights and rights claiming in these ways allows us to rethink or relocate what some describe as the "paradox of rights." The paradox of rights is not that rights claims work sometimes and fail sometimes, nor that they enable certain possibilities while constraining others. Instead, the paradox of rights is that we want the practice of making rights claims to end political debate, but at the same time we must recognize that their meaning and power actually derive from ongoing political engagement. Recognizing rights claiming as a practice of persuasion means embracing the fact that rights claiming is neither the representation of an absolute truth nor an activity whose felicity can be guaranteed. Instead, rights claiming is the activity of making equivocal utterances and of presenting perspectives that may or may not be embraced by the community to which they are made. If Mill's work reveals that rights claiming is not a trumping but, rather, a persuasive activity, it reminds us, then, of the importance of ongoing political engagement.

4

Claiming Rights and Performing Citizenship

Introduction

One arena in which there is considerable evidence that rights claiming is a highly uncertain and extraordinarily frustrating practice of persuasion that requires ongoing political engagement is the debate over same-sex marriage in California. Twice now—in the fall of 2000 and again in 2008—the citizens of the state have voted to define marriage as the union between one man and one woman and thus to reserve the right to marriage for opposite-sex couples.[1] At the same time, the State Supreme Court and a federal district court have ruled that such a law is at odds with the dictates of the state's constitution.[2] While judges may be persuaded that same-sex couples have a right to marry under California's equal protection clause, a majority of citizens in the state are not. Whether California will join the more than thirty states that expressly prohibit the right of same-sex couples to marry or whether it will become one of a handful of states in the nation to recognize it, only time will tell. As the case of *Perry v. Schwarzenegger* makes its way through the court system, however, the debate has much to tell us about the complicated relationship between rights and democracy, as well as about the value, and possible limits, of making rights claims to advance democratic ends, whatever these may be. In this chapter, I take a closer look at rights claiming occurring in the context of same-sex marriage debates in California, not in order to determine which legal or moral arguments are "correct," as in most consistent with the Constitution, rooted in the fundamental principles on which the United States was founded, or grounded in a universally accepted moral teaching. Instead, my point is to read the debate from the perspective of performativity developed in the preceding chapters, and to illustrate how it is that understanding rights claims as performative utterances brings to light important aspects of their democratic character obscured by more traditional approaches. This means, then, that I explore not only what we do when we make a claim to the right to marry members of the same sex but also what we do when, in opposing same-sex marriage, we may make a claim to a right to self-governance.

In addition, I use the same-sex marriage debate as a way to investigate a slightly different concern about the tensions between rights and democracy than addressed in the previous chapters. To be sure, the debate over same-sex marriage rights raises significant questions about whether rights are fundamentally anti-democratic when they are used to challenge majoritarian decision making: Is a judge who recognizes a right to same-sex marriage and rules a popularly decided policy initiative unconstitutional undermining the will of the people and illegitimately taking up the role of policy maker? It certainly raises concerns about the way we think of ourselves as rights-bearing subjects in the context of a democratic community: Is someone fighting for the right to same-sex marriage simply expressing an individual desire that disregards concerns about the public good? Or is someone who defends the right of citizens to self-governance brushing aside a democratic commitment to equality? And the case clearly challenges the association of rights with trumps: If a court's decision is not the last word on a subject, and if the legitimacy of a courtroom victory can be challenged by the people themselves, what will ever guarantee that a right will be recognized or enforced? At the same time, however, the debate raises issues that exceed the bounds of what we might identify as the liberal-communitarian debates about and the deliberative democratic approaches to rights.[3] Indeed, it brings into sharp focus concerns raised by scholars influenced by the writings of thinkers such as Karl Marx and Michel Foucault and associated with different strands of feminist thought, queer theory, and critical legal studies. These scholars worry less about whether rights claiming is a trumping practice that perpetuates an ethos of atomistic individualism and more about the kind of power rights claiming entails or enables. They raise concerns about the ideological and disciplinary dimensions of rights discourse, shedding light on how rights claiming enhances the regulatory power of the state often through the expansion of capitalism and the production and entrenchment of particular forms of identity that are profoundly depoliticizing. As I argue in this chapter, appreciating the performative dimensions of rights claiming in all of its complexity shows us how and why such concerns are overstated.

Debating Prop 8

As I suggested above, the debate over same-sex marriage rights heated up in California during the fall of 2008, when citizens were asked to vote on a referendum amending the state constitution to read that "Only marriage between a man and a woman is valid or recognized in California." Though the referendum, commonly referred to as Prop 8, passed with 52 percent of the vote, it was subsequently ruled unconstitutional by a federal district judge in 2010, and this ruling is currently under appeal.[4] On the face of it, the debate over Prop 8 seems to take place in fairly traditional terms that pit a commitment to individual or minority rights against the decisions of democratic majorities. This is expressed, quite often, in the claim made by opponents of same-sex marriage rights that "activist" judges are usurping the will of the people by making decisions that overrule democratically decided measures. Additionally, opponents argue that advocates for same-sex marriage rights are placing the protection of individual liberty ahead of the public good that results from building a nation upon and stabilized by procreative marriages that provide children with a mother and a father. In response, advocates of same-sex marriage rights point out that because the California constitution provides equal protection to all of its citizens, denying same-sex couples the right to marry is a fundamentally unconstitutional form of discrimination that is at odds with the democratic commitment to equality and fairness. Rather than threatening the health of a democratic community, granting same-sex couples the right to marry, advocates argue, advances the health of our nation by expanding the possibilities for loving and committed families.[5] Given these arguments, we might think of the two sides as rehearsing a centuries-old debate about whether or not democracy is best advanced or likely undermined by a focus on protecting rights. Nonetheless, reducing the debate to concerns about the counter-majoritarian nature of rights—that is, seeing it as a conflict between a commitment either to rights or to the will of the people—belies the complexity of the arguments marshaled by both sides in the fight and ignores an important set of arguments that come from those on the political left who may oppose same-sex marriage while remaining committed to identifying and eradicating inequalities in the lives of gays and lesbians. At the same time, it tells us almost nothing about what we do in and through the practice of making rights claims whether for or against same-sex marriage. If, however, we treat rights claims as performative utterances rather than as representations of legal fact or moral truth, as claims of persuasion that represent perspectives that may or may not influence the behavior and thought of others rather than as trumping claims that will, if uttered under the proper circumstances, guarantee some particular outcome, a great deal more becomes visible. In particular, we see that it is in and through claiming the right to marry that both opponents and proponents of same-sex marriage envision, enact, and contest good citizenship.[6]

Good citizenship, of course, neither looks the same for those who oppose same-sex marriage and those who support it nor is it reducible to one particular practice or way of being for either side. In fact, reading the debate about same-sex marriage through the lens of performativity illuminates the sometimes competing and sometimes overlapping versions of citizenship proffered by the two sides. Those who oppose same-sex marriage in California, for example, make their case by defending both the right of opposite-sex couples to marry and the right of the people to be self-governing, and each claim, in turn, carries with it a somewhat different vision of the good citizen. In arguing that there is no fundamental right to same-sex marriage, only a right for members of the opposite-sex to marry, opponents of same-sex marriage depict good citizenship as entailing participation in the age-old tradition of marrying in order to reproduce and raise children. Those members of the opposite sex who exercise their right to marry are said to provide a vital service, perhaps even a duty, to society by begetting the next generation of citizens and caring for these children in the kinds of stable and nurturing homes that produce healthy, productive, and responsible members of society. To claim that opposite-sex couples have a right to marry is, then, to present a vision of a nation stabilized and advanced by the work of traditional nuclear families. In making this claim, however, opponents of same-sex marriage do far more than simply present their perspectives on good citizenship: they also enact it. In other words, claiming that the right to marry be limited to members of the opposite sex can be understood as both a perlocutionary and illocutionary utterance. In the first case, rights claiming presents a perspective that, though it is designed to engage the sentiments and reason of listeners, may or may not be persuasive to others and may or may not influence their feelings and behaviors. In the second case, the very political act of claiming marriage rights for opposite-sex couples does (or at least attempts to do) the work of protecting children from the supposedly pernicious effects of thinking that same-sex marriage is acceptable. As backers of Proposition 8 wrote in the 2008 "California Voter Information

Guide," by supporting a proposition to define marriage as a union between one man and one woman, parents actually prevent their children from harmful exposure to values they find disagreeable.[7] At the same time, opponents of same-sex marriage rights, at least in California, marshal another argument that offers and enacts a slightly different vision of exemplary citizenship. This comes out in the claim that Proposition 8 protects the fundamental right of citizens to be self-governing. Here, the good citizen is the one who, married or not, takes an active role in the policymaking process and thus accepts responsibility for influencing the future of the society. In defending the restriction of marriage rights to opposite-sex couples, opponents of same-sex marriage recognize and embrace the privilege and importance of civic participation, and through their claims, they refuse to sit back and allow the government to make the decisions for them. The claim to protecting the right of self-governance, in its perlocutionary and illocutionary dimensions, thus enacts a form of exemplary citizenship in which the good citizen is a member of a larger community—"the people"—composed of individuals capable of determining, or of having determined, what is best for society.[8]

Of course, advocates for same-sex marriage rights present and perform a somewhat different vision of good citizenship in and through their rights arguments. In making an equal protection argument, for example, advocates for same-sex marriage rights suggest that the good citizen is one who welcomes difference into the community and embraces nontraditional family forms.[9] In and by making a claim to this right, same-sex couples and their advocates perform a version of citizenship that explicitly challenges and expands the way we conceive of and participate in spousal and familial relationships. But the claim does more than that: it also reveals a good citizen who shares quite a bit in common with the citizen championed by those who oppose same-sex marriage rights. In other words, though the gender combination of the married couples would be different, and thus the vision of married citizens in the United States transformed, the fundamental nature of the spousal relationship seems to remain the same for both opponents and proponents of same-sex marriage. As supporters of same-sex marriage rights explain, couples who seek the various benefits accorded by state and social recognition of their spousal relationships do so because they are engaged in the kind of loving and committed relationships that opponents believe form the bedrock of social stability.[10] Defenders of the right of same-sex couples to marry explicitly acknowledge that the spousal relationships they seek to have legitimated are those entered into by mature, committed, and loving adults who, quite often, have the explicit purpose of raising children and take their responsibility to each other and the next generation seriously. Indeed, for many advocates of same-sex marriage rights, the very right to marry symbolizes, makes possible, and even enacts a loving choice and a universal desire for commitment. Providing support for the centrality of love and commitment to the struggle for same-sex marriage rights, the National Gay and Lesbian Task Force Foundation explains in their *amicus* brief filed in *Perry v. Schwarzenegger* that:

> Little ink need be spilled establishing marriage's immense social value, as attested to by many of the witnesses at trial. Marriage has been described as "an institution of transcendent historical, cultural and social significance." The California Supreme Court likewise acknowledged "the long and celebrated history of the term 'marriage'"; "the widespread understanding that this term describes a union unreservedly approved and favored by the community"; and the "considerable and undeniable symbolic importance to this designation."[11]

Here, then, advocates of same-sex marriage rights reinforce the idea that the good citizen is a married citizen raising children in a home with a committed partner even while they expand our very ability to imagine what this married couple or a family looks like. In this way, claiming a right to same-sex marriage simultaneously transforms aspects of marriage while positioning same-sex couples as regular people who want and care about the same things as respectable and monogamous opposite-sex couples.[12]

Such complicated perspectives on and enactments of citizenship are obscured when one treats the debate as a contest over and effort to achieve legal, moral, or political accuracy; when one reduces it to a dispute over what is best for children or what the Constitution truly means; or when one focuses solely on determining how a particular rights claim should be made to guarantee its trumping capacity. But what is gained by shedding light on the performative dimensions of rights claiming, as I did above, by treating the claim to marriage rights as a perlocutionary and illocutionary utterance? The value of such an analysis of rights claiming lies, in part, in the way it draws our attention to the different and sometimes inconsistent ways in which the practice of rights claiming imagines and performs good citizenship. Additionally, it encourages, perhaps even demands, that we understand rights claiming as a practice of persuasion that, in its perlocutionary dimensions, is full of peril and promise. A performative analysis of the kind offered above also explicitly challenges us to loosen our attachment to the idea that rights claiming is either a simple representation of facts about the world or a practice that, for better or worse, should and can be like throwing a trump in a game of cards. These are the themes I illuminate in the following section.

The Problems and Promise of Claiming Same-Sex Marriage Rights

Recognition of the performativity of rights claiming may not provide political solace to those who seek to put an end to a form of injustice or instance of the usurpation of power once and for all. It does not tell us, for example, which vision of citizenship is to be preferred in the case of the same-sex marriage debates or which will be more persuasive to the judiciary and to the public. And while this may be troubling for those who seek to make rights claiming a felicitous speech activity that will have a clearly definable political effect, this is not the greatest concern for a different group of rights critics: those on the political left. Unlike the rights scholars associated with the liberal and deliberative democratic traditions discussed earlier in the book, these Left critics are concerned less with determining which felicity conditions must be met in order to produce a procedurally or ethically acceptable or legitimate rights claims than with shedding light on the ways in which rights claiming expands the regulatory power of the state and constitutes gay and lesbian individuals in particularly limiting ways. In addition, Left scholars and activists may be extremely skeptical about the value of making claims for same-sex marriage rights, but they are, nevertheless, wholly committed to ending the discrimination and injustices that gays and lesbians experience. And, it is because of this commitment that they worry about the constitutive or generative capacities of the practice of rights claiming that a performative approach to rights claiming celebrates. However, as I argue below, though the Left critiques of same-sex marriage may do the important work of drawing our attention to the potentially problematic effects of rights claiming, they also underestimate the democratic potential of rights claiming—in part because they misrepresent the disciplinary power of the practice itself. Indeed, the Left critiques, like the rights-as-trumps approach, obscures the unpredictability that is at the heart of both language use and political practice. This becomes evident when we read the work of Left critics such as Michael Warner and Wendy Brown both with and against the writings of Michel Foucault.

In his well-known text, *The Trouble with Normal,* Warner offers an early and influential version of what I am calling the Left critique of same-sex marriage rights. According to Warner's argument, prioritizing the fight for same-sex marriage rights may have the unfortunate effect of actually constraining rather than advancing the sexual and personal freedom and creativity of gay and lesbian individuals. "As long as people marry," he writes, "the state will continue to regulate the sexual lives of those who do not marry. It will continue to refuse to recognize our intimate relations—including cohabitating partnerships—as having the same rights or validity as a married couple."[13] Warner's concern here, with its echoes of earlier feminist critiques of marriage, is that in fighting for the right to same-sex marriage, gay couples reinforce the idea that normal and respectable intimate relationships result in marriage and family, and when measured against this norm, all other relationships will be found wanting.[14] The result of a preoccupation with winning same-sex marriage rights will be, Warner argues, to delegitimize, if not demonize or even criminalize, alternative family forms and sexual relationships, and such outcomes are decidedly at odds with the aims of gay liberation. In addition, Warner worries that such a focus can be profoundly distracting, even depoliticizing, particularly to the extent that it renders care for family and children, and the future of the nation, a responsibility of private families. Explaining this concern, he writes that:

> any politics based on such a sentimental rhetoric of privacy is not only a false idealization of love and coupling; it is an increasingly powerful way of distracting citizens from the real, conflicted, and unequal conditions governing their lives, and . . . it serves to reinforce the privilege of those who already find it easiest to imagine their lives as private.[15]

Warner's concerns about the normalizing effects of making claims for same-sex marriage rights should be taken seriously because they are neither unfounded nor unique. As we can see from the arguments presented in the Proposition 8 debates, advocates for same-sex marriage rights certainly present the loving, committed, responsible same-sex couple as the norm, and celebrate this relationship to the exclusion of others. In addition, Warner is correct that both opponents and proponents of same-sex marriage rights, in depicting marriage as the institution which not only celebrates love and commitment but also ensures the health and well-being of children and the nation, tend to erase the economic and social factors that make such flourishing possible.

These are, however, not the only problems that Left critics of rights claiming illuminate. Wendy Brown, for example, argues that when rights claims are made on behalf of members of particular identity groups, such as women, gays and lesbians, or other individuals who share some identity or experience, they often reference and reinforce the idea that the claimant is a victim of the state or society and implicitly presume that winning the right is the solution to the problem. In the end, such rights claiming ends up enacting and entrenching a particularly problematic conception of identity. As Brown explains, when we call attention to the specific injuries that the denial of certain rights has on particular individuals, we codify understandings of gender and sexuality that then "imprison us within the subject positions [rights] are secured to affirm or protect."[16] Rights claiming, in other words, reinforces our investment in our own status as victims as well as marks our participation in the creation and perpetuation of norms of victimization that become extraordinarily difficult to challenge.[17] To a certain extent, Brown's perspective would seem to capture something important about the same-sex marriage rights claims: making a claim to equal protection does position same-sex couples as victims of discrimination, as individuals who have been unfairly and unjustly denied both the material and the social benefits associated with the state's legitimation of one's intimate relationship. If Brown is correct, then, winning a right to have their marriages legitimated by the state and society—the clearly desired goal of the legal and political campaign for these rights—would in turn reinforce same-sex couples' attachment to this injury and reify the norms associated with being a victim of discrimination.[18] It would certainly not address the myriad other ways in which same-sex couples experience discrimination or inequality; that is, limiting state power in the arena of sexual relations does not necessarily reduce and may actually increase the way in which power works through other institutions and techniques to regulate the sexual acts and identities of individuals. In fact, winning particular rights, Brown's argument suggests, would only provide the illusion of having made progress toward individual freedom, sovereign subjectivity, and state responsiveness all the while increasing the scope of the state power and the prevalence of regulatory social norms. Rights claiming, from Brown's perspective, should be understood, then, as a practice that entrenches individuals in normative identity categories, which in turn requires that we let go of our attachment to rights claiming to a degree.

Brown's contention that we loosen our attachment to identity-based rights claims such as the right to same-sex marriage rests on a second concern that has to do with the kind of politics generated by a focus on identity. The problem with identity-based rights claiming, she argues, is not simply that it entrenches individuals in identity categories that increase state power but also that feelings of victimization expressed by the rights claimant give rise to a politics of *ressentiment* marked by moralizing, righteousness, blame, and a desire for punishment.[19] When winning rights comes to stand for freedom, when instrumentally effective rights arguments come to signify political action, the result is a transformation of "the instrumental function of law into a political end" and the "bartering of political freedom for legal protection."[20] This practice of claiming rights on behalf of victimized identity groups, in turn, undermines a participatory democratic politics; it makes it less likely, in other words, that "humans govern themselves by governing together."[21] Whether Brown is correct that claiming same-sex marriage rights will give or has given rise to a particularly instrumental and moralizing form of politics is, of course, a matter of interpretation, and perhaps something we will be able to fully assess only when those rights have been won across the nation. Her suggestion that we should not confuse legal recognition with emancipation nor underestimate the importance of ongoing political engagement remains, nonetheless, an important one. Heeding this warning, however, need not entail a rejection of making rights claims. Indeed, as I suggest below, to follow the Left critique of rights to its logical conclusion would be to make both a political and a philosophical mistake.[22]

Politically, we can see that the fight for same-sex marriage rights is not simply a matter of presenting oneself as a victim of discrimination. To be sure, that is an important part of the argument: same-sex couples, even those who have state-recognized civil unions, because they do not get the same legal or social benefits as married couples, are thus harmed by the denial of these rights. A focus on the harm, however, misses the extent to which same-sex married couples remain as active participants in the process of cultivating the next generation of democratic citizens nonetheless. While such a perspective may unnecessarily and unfortunately privatize that process, as well as circumscribe our understanding of what a married couple is, it nonetheless requires seeing spouses in a marriage as capable of having significant responsibilities and making important judgments, of seeing same-sex couples as active and engaged citizens. At the same time, to focus attention on the negative effects of rights claiming underestimates the work that rights claiming does to bring often previously disenfranchised people together, to give them voice, and to allow them to shape the future of a community.

Philosophically, an emphasis on the negative effects of rights claiming unnecessarily reduces the performative capacities of rights claiming and misrepresents disciplinary power. This is not to suggest that a Left critique of rights is philosophically incorrect but, rather, to suggest that it is incomplete. In drawing attention to the potentially pernicious effects of rights claiming, critics forget something that Foucault himself acknowledges—that rights claiming, perhaps because it entails a degree of unpredictability and contingency of outcomes like any other speech activity, may actually have transformative effects. In emphasizing the ways that disciplinary power constrains and regulates, Left critiques of rights claiming obscure this potential. That is not to suggest that Foucault celebrates rights-based political efforts. He certainly does argue that when one makes rights claims, one is usually turning to the state for recognition and redress of specific kinds of injuries. Rights, in this scenario, he cautions, are presumed to fix the limits of legitimate state and social power in a way that actually fails to account for the complexity of contemporary forms of power. Power, he explains, circulates "at the extremities," through nonstate, nonjuridical institutions, locations, and techniques, and a traditional understanding of the relationship between rights claiming and state power misses this, obscuring the extent to which power works through techniques of surveillance and normalization that far exceed the reach of the juridical edifice. We see an insight such as this expressed in Warner's claim that winning a right to same-sex marriage may lead neither to the freedom of gays and lesbians nor to a future in which the state mandates that gay and lesbian couples marry. Rather, it may lead to the increasingly accepted social norm that defines married gays as "good" gays. Here, Warner draws on a Foucauldian notion of disciplinary power to remind us that rights claiming both produces and reinforces that which is taken to be normal and natural.

I suggest, however, that we read Foucault in light of his own political activism and embrace of rights claiming. In other words, Foucault should not be read as completely rejecting rights; indeed, he recognizes their democratic potential, particularly when they are understood anew: "If one wants . . . to struggle against disciplines and disciplinary power, it is not towards the ancient right of sovereignty that one should turn, but to a new form of right, one which must indeed be anti-disciplinarian, but at the same time liberated from the principle of sovereignty."[23] In fact, he goes so far as to suggest that if rights claims are made to challenge norms rather than to reinforce or restrict traditionally conceived state power, and if we recognize that rights are not things that an individual has or that the state can simply protect, then their transformative potential may come to fruition. This means that rights claims need to be made in ways that expand the possibility of living, thinking, and acting differently in the future, thereby countering the tendency to reify already existing identity categories. With such an argument, Foucault makes a gesture toward the kinds of rights claiming I have been associating with perlocutionary utterances and the practice of persuasive politics.

Foucault does not spend significant time detailing the content of this "new form of right," but we can begin to see its relevance for thinking about rights claims as performative utterances when we explore some of the essays and interviews he gave not too long before his death. There, he began to develop the idea of a "relational right."[24] Foucault describes relational rights as those that recognize and create new ways for individuals to relate to each other. Such rights claims, like more traditional rights claims, entail "gaining recognition in an institutional sense for the relations of one individual to another individual"; yet, this is a recognition of something new: "It's a question of imagining how the relation of two individuals can be validated by society and benefit from the same advantages as the relations . . . which are the only ones recognized."[25] Relational rights, in other words, represent and constitute new ways of living that exceed the heretofore recognized possibilities. Rather than simply fitting oneself within the confines of existing ways of being and doing, relational rights involve the creation of new forms of relationships beyond those currently codified in the law and recognized by the state. As such, making claim to these rights is an act of refusing the ways in which we are traditionally defined and is an attempt to bring into existence new attitudes and enact new ways of living and relating to each other previously unrecognized or legitimated.[26] By way of illustration, Foucault suggests claiming a right for adult adoption—that is, a right for adults to adopt other adults. At the present time, he argues, we have no way of thinking about and understanding relationships of care and obligation among adults except in terms of marriage and the family. The right to adult adoption would question these accepted relationships while expanding the possibilities for living together and caring for others.[27] It would bring into existence a new way of understanding intimate relations of care and dependency, allowing us to "escape as much as possible from the type of relations that society proposes for us and try to create in the empty space . . . new relational possibilities."[28] And this "escape" would come not necessarily or only by way of legally sanctioned rights. In fact, Foucault imagines deploying the language of a right of adult adoption not simply to create state-sanctioned rights but also, and perhaps more important, to expand what counts as an acceptable relationship in realms beyond the state.[29] As Foucault suggests, by making rights claims in this way, directed at both the state and disciplinary norms, one challenges "the effects of power which are linked with knowledge, competence, and qualification," calling into question the very mechanisms by which identity categories are constituted and policed.[30]

Of importance for the issues at the heart of this book is the fact that Foucault's description of relational rights bears some resemblance to the kind of performativity I have identified in the calls for same-sex marriage rights. In both cases, rights claims present new perspectives on the world and question traditional norms and ways of being. To be sure, same-sex marriage rights claims may not be as radical as adult adoption rights, but they are, nonetheless, claims that challenge aspects of what we take to be normal and natural. The notion of relational rights thus not only points the way to an alternative understanding of the practice of rights claiming but also challenges Left critiques of rights' disciplinary character for downplaying—indeed, at times denying—rights' contestatory potential. This argument, of course, presupposes a particular theory of agency and resistance whereby discourse is not simply an effect of power but "a hindrance, stumbling block" to it as well.[31] It is rooted in an understanding of disciplinary power as that which, rather than extinguishing a subject's capacity for agency or foreclosing all possibility of freedom, makes that very freedom and resistance possible. As Foucault explains, "freedom must exist for power to be exerted . . . since without the possibility of recalcitrance, power would be equivalent to a physical determination."[32] Disciplinary power may produce us as particular subjects, but this production is neither totalizing nor seamless—and neither must it be wholly constraining. In fact, according to Foucault, disciplinary power produces us as subjects capable of freedom, capable of action, capable of resistance. That is not to deny that practices of resistance like rights claiming may entrench power, that the relationships and identities constituted through practices like adult adoption or same-sex marriage may be used to reinforce normalization. However, this, as Foucault reminds us, is not an adequate objection to the practices themselves. No language or practice of resistance can bring about the end to political debate and struggle, no matter how liberated from an ancient theory of sovereignty. The best a practice of freedom can do is to protect or create "the political, social, and cultural conditions under which individuals are allowed the possibility of struggling to change these same conditions."³³ And this is precisely what relational rights do: they work to resist and refuse the imposition and naturalization of identity. As such, they are one aspect of anti-disciplinary, agonistic politics of resistance, a politics of "reciprocal incitation and struggle; less of a face-to-face confrontation which paralyzes both sides than a permanent provocation."³⁴

Reclaiming Identity for Democratic Politics

But how does this process of transformation, this provocation that is itself a resignification, actually work? To explore this process in more detail— and to draw out the insight of speech act theory that utterances are often acts that produce the very speaking subjects they seem to presume—I draw on insights from the work of Judith Butler and return to the work of Hannah Arendt. Both thinkers, I suggest, shed light on how identity-based claims, whether they are specifically rights claims or not, constitute and reconstitute our very sense of self and the world in which we live. These thinkers thus provide a vocabulary or set of categories missing from but complementary to the insights of more traditional speech act theory and are thus helpful in shedding light on the democratic potential of rights claiming in the context of same-sex marriage debates.

I find Butler's work helpful for thinking about how a rights claim can transform ways of being in the world and expand possibilities for the future. Such transformation occurs, she explains, when rights claims juxtapose a universal to a particular or, more specifically, when the claim itself reveals a supposedly universal conception of identity to be premised upon the exclusion of precisely those who are making demands for inclusion. This happens, for example, in the international efforts to have gay rights recognized as human rights. Making international human rights claims for gays and lesbians, she explains, "is always in the process of subjecting the human to redefinition and renegotiation. It mobilizes the human in service of rights, but also rewrites the human and rearticulates the human when it comes up against the cultural limits of its working conception of the human."[35] In other words, to juxtapose gays and lesbians to humans and to demand that the former be included in the latter group is to simultaneously expose the category "human" as something other than universal and to make a claim for inclusion into a category— personhood—that gives it new meaning. This is a process of transformation or resignification rather than either repudiation or reification. Calling for gays and lesbians to be included in the category of persons who can claim international human rights disrupts a normative identity category, in part by offering an alternative vision of the future in a manner similar to Foucault's relational rights. Such claims to gay rights as human rights cannot, in other words, simply be reduced to calls for recognition of victimization or the reification of an already existing identity category particularly because, as Butler explains, such claims are made without the presumption that rights emanate from a specific attribute of our very being. What we see in the fight for the international human rights of gays and lesbians is that:

> we are not simply struggling for rights that attach to my person, but we are struggling *to be conceived as persons*. . . . If we are struggling for rights that attach, or should attach, to my personhood, then we assume that personhood as already constituted. But if we are struggling not only to be conceived as persons, but to create a social transformation of the very meaning of personhood, then the assertion of rights becomes a way of intervening into the social and political process by which the human is articulated.[36]

This is not, however, an uncomplicated practice. Indeed, Butler calls the work of making such rights claims a practice of "perverse reiteration" that entails both revealing the universal to be "limited and exclusionary" and "mobiliz[ing] a new set of demands."[37] By calling myself a name that I am not usually called—indeed, a name I am expected *not* to be called—I make a claim that is new and yet intelligible, both unfamiliar and familiar at the same time. My claiming is not a simple assimilation of the norm but, rather, a claim in which "we are confronted with a strange neighboring of the universal and the particular which neither synthesizes the two, nor keeps them apart."[38] In calling myself human when human is premised upon my exclusion, I both highlight that exclusion and suggest that the term can be understood in more inclusive ways. I challenge traditional understandings of the intelligible, helping to shape and expand possible ways of thinking and being. Through rights claiming, that is, we constitute our individual identities as well as our political communities in a paradoxical process that expands the conception of personhood by drawing attention to previously unauthorized conceptions of personhood: "assert[ing] a right or entitlement to a livable life when no such prior authorization exists, when no clearly enabling convention is in place."[39] Making rights claims thus entails avowing dependency—the norms that produce us—as well as challenging the status quo, for rights must be understood as a site of the contestation of the very meaning and possibility of personhood.

I would suggest that we see a similar, if somewhat less obvious, juxtaposition of the universal and the particular in the claims made by those seeking the right to same-sex marriage. If the married person is, as the opponents of same-sex marriage themselves acknowledge, often understood as a universally recognizable good democratic citizen, a responsible member of society who contributes to the stability and future productivity of the nation through the rearing of children, the claim to same-sex marriage rights exposes that particular understanding of citizenship as exclusive to opposite-sex couples. It also exposes the good married citizen as predominantly a reproducing or child-rearing individual. In both cases, the claim to include same-sex couples in the category of legitimately married citizens demands that we imagine marriage in new ways, with different individuals occupying the place of parents specifically while disaggregating marriage from procreation more generally. Without claims to same-sex marriage rights being made, we do not necessarily see the way the category of the married citizen is constituted or how it functions as a norm in our society, and thus we do not expand our ways of envisioning and enacting citizenship and spousal relationships. As a practice of perverse reiteration, claiming a right to same-sex marriage contributes to what Butler calls the "remaking [of] reality" and the expansion of the livable.[40] When gays and lesbians make claims to human rights, or the right to be married, such rights claims both reinforce and reshape the meaning of the rights-bearing subject. As Butler helps us to see, rights claiming thus reflects not the traditional liberal practice of claiming that one has a right by nature, the way one may have an arm or a leg, but, rather, that one is involved in a process of claiming to be conceived as a rights-bearing individual, as a person, in the first place. Here, then, rights claiming becomes a performative practice that is provocative in a Foucauldian sense, for it is through the claiming itself that we, as Butler puts it, make an intervention "into the social and political process by which the human is articulated."[41] If performative utterances are acts that constitute us as subjects, they are transformative in a positive sense when they allow us to imagine a different future and open up the space for us to become something other than we are.

This process of transformation or resignification does not and cannot simply disavow the facts of past injustice or injury. To do so, as Hannah Arendt suggests, would be crazy. This is what I take her to have suggested when, upon being awarded the Lessing Prize by the city of Hamburg, she accepted explicitly as a Jew. In her speech, Arendt pondered the fact that she, a Jew who only a few years earlier had been exiled from her country, a Jew who would not have been allowed to speak in public or celebrated as an important public intellectual, had been chosen as an exemplar of the humanist tradition. In considering the irony of her situation, Arendt challenged her audience to reconsider the meaning of humanism itself, particularly in light of the attitude and spirit with which Lessing approached life—his recognition that plurality is a vital component of creating humanity.[42] And thus, in what must have been a surprising move, Arendt explained that she would accept the award, but only by speaking as a Jew—not an abstract human being or world citizen, but as a member of a group whose religious identity had been used to justify their persecution.[43] Though it might seem odd that a thinker who very clearly rejected an ontological orientation to identity would feel compelled to "bluntly reveal the personal background of [her] reflections," to do otherwise, she suggested, would be to escape into "cloud-cuckoo-land."[44] With this statement, Arendt engaged in an act of perverse reiteration that revealed the performativity as well as the transformative capacity of identity-based claims. Understanding how this works in her speech can thus help us to see the continued value of referencing normative identity categories while claiming rights.

Arendt, we know, explicitly rejected the idea of identity as an attribute or a stable, pre-political aspect of a person's being. She believed that *who* someone is could not be captured by attributes such as biology or psychology. Instead this *who* is produced or results from active engagement in public life.[45] Here, Arendt hints at an understanding of identity that we might associate with theories of performativity, but it is one that also reminds us that the performative and constative need not be seen as opposed. That is, in claiming her identity as a Jew, she draws our attention to the limits of universals and to the important role that the particularities of identity have to play in politics. Indeed, her message in "On Humanity in Dark Times" is that there are times when making universal claims may be politically dangerous and give rise to "misunderstandings" that put politics and the very world that exists between individuals in jeopardy.[46] In "dark times," when the political realm is shrinking and relations between individuals are diminishing, resuscitating humanity and politics, Arendt seems to be suggesting, requires turning not to universals and celebrating a presumed sameness of individuals but, rather, acknowledging our unique and distinct places in the world. In dark times, "in times of defamation and persecution," political engagement requires resisting "in terms of the identity that is under attack."[47]

Of course, Arendt's embrace of her Jewish identity might seem to be precisely the kind of victimized identification that troubles Brown.[48] It would seem as if, in other words, the self-affirmation of one's complex identity served as the basis of or precondition for efficacious acts of political resistance, but this is not the case. Arendt not only rejects such an ontology but also cautions against unnecessarily juxtaposing universal personhood to specific identity while urging a rethinking of the very meaning of specificity. By recognizing her Jewish identity she made visible the fact that her Jewishness conditioned the way in which her actions were interpreted and her participation in the political realm was determined. Understanding identity as a political fact means recognizing the ways in which relations of power, institutions, and historical circumstances give meaning to identity categories that condition the possibilities of speaking and acting in public. When the fact of being differently positioned and conditioned by identity is acknowledged, rather than obscured, then the space of politics is created and it becomes possible to act and think differently. In dark times, for example, "under the conditions of the Third Reich, it would scarcely have been a sign of humanness for . . . friends to have said: Are we not both human beings? It would have been a mere evasion of reality and of the world common to both at the time . . ."[49] And, as Arendt explains, it is only when individuals acknowledge the political fact of their identities, only when the Jew and German meet and engage together as Jew and German, as individuals conditioned in different ways by historically contingent constructions of identity, that it becomes possible to resignify and reconstitute the meaning of an identity category, particularly one that has been used to subordinate. Through the explicit invocation of her Jewish identity, Arendt is able to acknowledge the power of a normative identity category at the same time that she exposes and challenges its status as a truth. She makes it possible to tell different stories about her own self and Jews in general, and this enables the disruption of norms. Acknowledging the fact of her identity is, then, part of a practice of "resisting the world as it was."[50]

Resisting in terms of the identity under attack is not, Arendt suggests, about making an ontological claim: "When I use the word 'Jew' I do not mean to suggest any special kind of human being."[51] Rather, to speak as a Jew is to acknowledge a "political fact," to shed light on a historical moment and a set of events, institutions, and relationships that conditioned the way individuals treated each other, to acknowledge "a political fact through which my being a member of this group outweighed all other questions of personal identity or rather had decided them in favor of anonymity, of namelessness."[52] To deny her Jewishness, or simply accept the award as an abstract human being or generic world citizen, would have been "nothing but a grotesque and dangerous evasion of reality," part of "the widespread tendency in Germany to act as though the years from 1933 to 1945 never existed."[53] It would have been an erasure of the realities of the world in which she lived and would have only contributed to the disappearance of the world between individuals. And thus, in bringing attention to past injury and specificity, Arendt is engaged in a decidedly political act that is both backward looking and future oriented, cognizant of the fact that possibilities for living differently in the future depend on the recognition, rather than the erasure, of past injustice.[54]

Arendt's recognition of identity as a political fact should be understood, then, as part of a contestatory performance of identity. By acting in public as a Jew, Arendt engages in the disclosure of her unique identity— "*Who* somebody is or was we can know only by knowing the story of which he is himself the hero"—that allows for the future disruption of norms, while reminding us that, under particular circumstances, this disruption, this resistance, requires an acknowledgment of the past.[55] By stressing her Jewishness, Arendt engages in a form of action that is meant to bring something new into existence. Her appreciation of identity as a political fact suggests that we can acknowledge injury and identity without being bound by them. Facts of identity can be made public without their being a claim about one's timeless and essential nature, without their serving as a narcissistic attachment to one's victimhood, and thus without the kind of *ressentiment* Brown so fears. By giving the facts that conditioned her existence narrative form, Arendt seeks not to "master the past" but, rather, to begin a process of reconciliation. Knowing what happened and "endur[ing] this knowledge," are necessary steps, she suggests, toward creating a better, albeit uncertain, future: We must "wait and see what comes of knowing and enduring."[56] And thus Arendt's appreciation of the political facticity of identity reminds us that identity claims are an important part of political resistance, a necessary but by no means perfectly emancipatory step in challenging relations of oppression and domination.[57] Appreciating "identity" as a political fact rather than as a natural and inevitable attribute has important consequences for thinking about the practice of rights claiming.

Arendt is not alone in recognizing that calling attention to past injury is an absolutely necessary part of the process of resignification. Butler does so as well. Indeed, she argues that "one of the central tasks of lesbian and gay international rights is to assert in clear and public terms the reality of homosexuality, not as an inner truth, not as a sexual practice, but as one of the defining features of the social world in its very intelligibility."[58] Here, she reminds us that norms of homosexuality make it possible for us to be intelligible as subjects, implying that there are and have been particular institutions, forms of knowledge, and relationships that have constituted our subjectivity, whether straight or gay, in particular ways. But she allows for the fact that this normalizing is not complete entrenchment. In fact, the very attachment to identity that Brown worries about becomes, on Butler's reading, an attachment that is necessary to both our formation as subjects and the possibility of our resistance to subjectification: "If . . . we understand certain kinds of interpellations to confer identity, those injurious interpellations will constitute identity through injury. This is not the same as saying that such an identity will remain always and forever rooted in its injury as long as it remains an identity, but it does imply that the possibilities of resignification will rework and unsettle the passionate attachment to subjection without which subject formation—and re-formation—cannot succeed."[59] We cannot, nor must we, deny the way identity categories normalize us; "our very individuality depends" upon that. Indeed, "the discourse of rights avows our dependency, the mode of being in the hands of others, a mode of being with and for others without which we cannot be."[60] And yet making these norms visible through rights, acknowledging that dependency, is a part of challenging these norms. For when we use rights language that acknowledges the facts of prior normalization, when we "assert an entitlement to conditions of life in ways that affirm the constitutive role of sexuality and gender in political life," we do not simply reify these facts. We have the opportunity to contest them as well, to "subject our very categories to critical scrutiny."[61] By drawing our attention to the way rights claiming allows us to resignify rather than simply reify identity, Butler helps us to see that the contestatory potential of rights need not require a complete refusal of identity or denial of our attachment to injury. Sometimes refusing what we are requires that we acknowledge what we have been understood to be. This practice of treating identity as a political fact and yet not denying its performativity is something that Arendt understood well and something that may be helpful for considering the ongoing value of making not just rights claims but also identity-based rights claims.

In bringing attention to the transformative potential of identity claims deployed in Arendt's speech, I am offering another way to think about and an additional reason to embrace rights claims made on behalf of particular identity groups. I do not, however, mean to suggest that identity-based rights claiming should be the sum total of a democratic politics. Indeed, the process of resignifying identity is not foolproof. Just because I say that those who have been traditionally excluded from human rights are actually rights-bearing subjects, or that same-sex couples are good citizens, does not mean that my claim will be understood. Such claims can certainly go unheard or be rejected. They can even be considered simply nonsensical. Indeed, as Butler acknowledges, the excessive character of language means that a doing or a saying that seems to replicate existing norms may be deemed unintelligible or incomprehensible at times. There is no guarantee, in other words, that my utterance, my rights claim, even if it does cite already existing norms, will be acknowledged, understood, or accepted as a repetition of those norms. Nor is there any guarantee that my utterance, even if intelligible, will engender subversive or progressive outcomes. Thus, embracing a performative understanding of a practice such as rights claiming will always entail a double movement. If we take performativity seriously, we must also engage in practices of critical self-reflection that call into question the presuppositions, expectations, and even outcomes of our practices. The need for critical scrutiny, however, does not mean rejecting problematic practices altogether. As Butler explains, engaging in critical scrutiny involves freeing a concept or practice "from its metaphysical lodgings in order to understand what political interests were secured in and by that metaphysical placing." This is not the same as doing away with the term or practice; in fact, it is to open up the space for the term or practice "to occupy and to serve very different political aims."[62]

Making rights claims, or making identity-based rights claims, certainly will not be able to address the myriad techniques through which subordination is practiced; no single theoretical advance or political technique will accomplish that. The orientation to identity-based rights claiming that I have detailed recognizes that resignification is always a risky project, and innovation and change can be both positive and negative, for "terms are never finally and fully tethered to a single use," whether progressive or subordinating. Instead, "they assume a life and a purpose that exceed the uses to which they have been consciously put."[63] And a recognition of this excess, of the uncontrollability of language, demands that we keep sight of the importance of making judgments. But before we turn to the issue of judgment, a few more illustrations of a performative analysis of rights claiming, and its implications for democratic theory and practice, are in order.

Making Rights Claims in the Age of AIDS

Introduction

As I have been suggesting throughout this book, rights claiming is, or at least can be, a form of political engagement that creates and contests the boundaries of community and the meaning of identity. It is a particularly democratic form of engagement when it makes this possible for people who, in some way or another, have been displaced from or find themselves on the outskirts of their particular communities, often without voice and more often without rights. Rights claiming, in these cases, is a valuable performative practice because it allows for the creation of a form of political subjectivity. This has been and continues to be particularly important in the age of AIDS.

Perhaps nowhere are the oddities of the relationship between rights and democracy more apparent than in the AIDS epidemic. Here, despite ongoing concerns that a focus on rights might undermine the interests of majorities and threaten the well-being of community, rights claiming has become an integral part of international political rhetoric and strategy; and despite concerns that certain rights claims perpetuate pernicious conceptions of victimized identity, identity-based rights claims are also flourishing. Indeed, demands for and efforts at responding to the prevention and treatment needs of HIV-infected and at-risk individuals have been framed more and more in terms of rights, particularly the rights of distinct groups of individuals. Depending on the specific policy and issue at hand, advocates for those living with and affected by HIV/AIDS make claims for everything from the rights to privacy and informed consent to the rights to be protected from discrimination, have access to treatment and affordable medical care, and be free from sexual violence, and they do so on behalf of homosexuals and hemophiliacs, women and the poor, sex workers and people of color. So pervasive and important is the language of rights to addressing the AIDS crisis that the United Nations adopted a Declaration of Commitment on HIV/AIDS in 2001 designating an effective response to the epidemic as a human right.

Of course, the ubiquity of rights claims made to demand, frame, or justify responses to the problems of HIV/AIDS should not be mistaken for consensus on what is to be done and why. Like the other rights controversies mentioned in this book, efforts to shape AIDS policy and law raise significant questions about the meaning and status of rights in the context of societies that claim or aspire to be democratic. For example, in the early days of the epidemic, when the disease appeared to affect mainly gay men, countries such as the United States worried that protecting the rights of infected and at-risk individuals might actually jeopardize the greater public health. This was particularly true with respect to debates about privacy rights where the concern was that allowing an individual to keep his HIV status private would compromise efforts to control and contain the spread of the disease. But even today, now that more than 30 million people are living with HIV/AIDS—and thus the distinctions between minority groups and the general public are far less clear—concerns about the conflicts between a commitment to rights and the advancement of democratic ends, values, and practices remain. In a world of limited resource, policymakers and activists continue to debate whether the rights of those infected should take precedence over the needs and interests of those who are uninfected or vice versa. They disagree about whether maintaining the confidentiality of one's status is more or less important than notifying an individual's sexual partners. They debate whether access to costly drug regimens designed to treat but unable to cure HIV/AIDS is a good use of limited financial and public health resources. And they worry that even when there is a stated commitment to protecting the rights of HIV-positive and at-risk individuals, effective practice and policy are extraordinarily difficult to ensure.

Such controversies reveal a concern not only with the possible antimajoritarian character of making rights claims in the age of AIDS, but also about the desirability and efficacy of a rights-based response to the crisis. What kind of people, some wonder, demand a right to privacy when the health and safety of others are at stake? What kind of society, others ask, focuses its efforts on legal change when the lives of millions of people are rendered far more vulnerable by the greed of multinational

pharmaceutical companies and the realities of a lack of decent employment opportunities? And even those who are far more comfortable with
the rights-based activism and framing that dominate AIDS policy debates
raise concerns about whether or not rights claims are really working effectively. In addition, rights claiming in the age of AIDS raises concerns
about the presuppositions and implications of the kind of identity-based
politics discussed in the previous chapter. When rights claims are made
on behalf of not only HIV-positive individuals but also specific segments
of this population (gay men, poor women, blacks, sex workers, etc.), questions arise about the potentially depoliticizing effect of such an approach,
and about what it might mean and what it might do to make a rights claim
on behalf of HIV-positive or at-risk individuals who may or may not claim
one or more of these particular labels.

Of course, given what I have been suggesting about the performativity
of language in general and rights claiming in particular, it is also important
to ask about what is made possible in and through these identity-based
rights claims. As I argue below, rights claiming in the age of AIDS challenges our understandings of who is a member of the general rights-bearing
public, and it reimagines what it can look like to live and thrive in the face
of illness. Indeed, rights claiming, particularly when it is done by those who
have HIV/AIDS, provides an opportunity for the creation of new forms of
political subjectivity. This is the process whereby people who have no place
or voice in a political community act as if they have both and, in doing so,
shift the basic understandings and boundaries of that community. This is
not a practice whereby an already formed group simply finds its voice or
embraces and re-presents an already given and stable identity. Instead, as
Jacques Rancière explains, the creation of political subjectivity comes about
and democratic politics itself comes into existence when "those who have
no right to be counted as speaking beings make themselves of some account," when they reconstitute community by placing a wrong in common
that reveals "the contradiction of two worlds in a single world: the world
where they are and the world where they are not."[1] Such an approach to
understanding the ways in which political subjectivity comes into being
takes seriously the idea that speaking and acting, even when that activity is
neither necessarily comprehensible nor formally authorized, generates
the possibility for and enables the transformation of democracy.

To shed light on the ways in which the practice of rights claiming in
the context of AIDS is a performative practice that generates a new political subjectivity, I focus my attention on one particular AIDS policy

controversy: the debate over policies designed to prevent mother-to-child (MTCT) HIV transmission. In the United States, this debate involved differing perspectives on whether or not to mandate HIV testing for all women of childbearing age, only for pregnant women, for newborns, or for some combination of these groups. Proponents of mandatory testing touted such policies as good public health practice and a means to protect the rights of newborns. While seemingly commonsensical on first glance, as I illustrate below, justifications for these policies rested on health-care arguments or rights claims that effectively excluded a large portion of women of childbearing from the political community, denying them not just their rights but also their voice. Mandatory testing proponents did this, in part, through speech acts depicting HIV-positive women as bad mothers who posed a threat to the public's physical and moral health. In response to this, opponents of mandatory testing made a variety of rights claims that, as I show, worked to refigure HIV-positive women as good mothers and give otherwise excluded women a voice in the community.

In South Africa, the debate over mother-to-child HIV transmission policies took a slightly different direction. Here, the focus was on whether or not HIV-positive women had a right to access to health care—that is, whether or not the South African government had a constitutional obligation to distribute potentially life-saving AIDS drugs to pregnant women and newborns. Rather than trying to limit the scope of state power through recourse to rights, women in South Africa made rights claims to demand action on the part of the state. Despite these important differences, advocates for the rights of HIV-positive women in both South Africa and the United States were actively engaged in a practice of envisioning and enacting forms of democratic community that could embrace pregnant women and mothers as citizens while recognizing women as individuals with distinct needs of their own. The comparison across countries thus reminds that rights claiming may always be a performative practice, but the nuances and significance of this activity become visible when we look at rights claims made in specific contexts.

The Threat of Bad Mothers

Public health crises have never been times in which the rights of individuals—particularly those who are already ill—are given high priority. The AIDS epidemic has been both a continuation of and an exception to this rule. In the early years of the epidemic in the United States, for example, individuals or groups infected with HIV or at risk of infection were often separated, sometimes literally and often figuratively, from the rest of the population because they were seen as posing a threat to the general public. The identification of certain people or groups as a health threat often coincided with and justified the curtailment and containment of these individuals through the suspension of various rights and, to a great extent, the silencing of their voices. What makes the AIDS epidemic unique, however, is that in many cases the infected and the vulnerable have fought back. Despite efforts to mute their voices or to declare their claims nonsensical, HIV-infected and at-risk individuals, in coalition with legal experts, rights activists, and public health officials, acted as if they could be heard, as if they had a part in the shaping of the community, and they did this through the making of rights claims. Though perhaps less visible than gay activists, HIV-positive and at-risk women, particularly those of child-bearing age, have been central to this practice. This comes as a result of new policies as well as ongoing health practices that compromised this particular group of women's status as members of the community.

In 1987, when it became clear that as many as 30 percent of HIV-infected women could transmit HIV to their infants (in utero, during delivery, or through breast milk), public health officials and policymakers became extremely worried about preventing the spread of infection to children. Dr. C. Everett Koop, then U.S. Surgeon General, called on medical professionals to craft a policy that would alleviate "the tremendous burden of this devastating condition, especially among children."[2] For many policymakers that meant implementing policies that would require women of childbearing age—or at least pregnant women and women in populations vulnerable to infection—to be tested for the virus. Such policies were thought to be necessary, life-saving measures that were consistent with traditional regulatory state responses to public health crises. As supporters explained, if HIV-infected women could be identified, efforts could be made both to help them avoid transmission (either through the termination of the pregnancy or by avoiding breastfeeding) and to get medical attention to newborns. In addition to touting the potential health benefits of mandatory testing, supporters defended these policies as very minor incursions into women's lives.[3] Mandatory HIV testing would be just one other test in the routine prenatal care of pregnant women, one addition to the numerous diseases and birth defects for which pregnant women were already tested, and one more health policy meant to protect the community from harm.[4]

With attention focused primarily on the prevention of mother-to-child HIV transmission (MTCT), women's own illness and risk were rendered practically invisible; their presence and importance in the epidemic reduced to their role as transmitters of the disease, as vessels and vectors of contagion.[5] These women were not, in other words, recognized as members of the general public who were in need of either public health services or the protection of their rights. It was not simply their illness, their vulnerability to illness, or even their status as pregnant women or potential mothers that rendered their distinct needs somewhat incomprehensible: it was the fact that they were—or had the potential to be—bad mothers. In other words, justifications for the policies to prevent mother-to-child HIV transmission rested on depictions of women as both medical and moral contagions, as bad mothers, as they had in prior public health crises. And such depictions, in turn, silenced the voices and obscured the needs of many HIV-positive women.

The media and the public health community played important roles in this process. Newspaper stories, particularly in the late 1980s and early 1990s, repeatedly scrutinized the actions and decisions of HIV-positive pregnant women in ways that reinforced the idea that women threatened the public health by being potential vectors of contagion. According to some newspaper accounts, for example, HIV-positive women were regularly being advised about the risks of perinatal HIV transmission and counseled to be tested before becoming pregnant, to use condoms to avoid pregnancy, and, at times, to have abortions if pregnant. And yet, or so the reports suggested, many HIV-positive women were failing to heed this advice, "react[ing] with passivity and denial [and] not using condoms."[6] HIV-positive women were presented as failing to account for the "dire new consequences" that a "freely chosen" and "unrestrained sexual life" would have on children.[7] By suggesting that women had the information and resources available to make different choices and take different actions, and simply refused to do so, the media presented HIV-positive pregnant women as willfully and knowingly engaging in irresponsible behavior. These women, the articles suggested, were needlessly and recklessly exposing their children to harm, and posing both a medical and a moral threat to the general welfare.

Like the media, the public health community often conflated the medical threat posed by HIV with a moral one. Dr. James Curran of the Centers for Disease Control (CDC), for example, called the rationality of HIV-positive women's opposition to the policy into question when he suggested that a pregnant woman "who understands the disease and is logical will not want to be pregnant and will consider the test results when making family planning decisions."[8] Such sentiments were expressed by other public health officials, who admitted that "health care practitioners who care for children find it especially difficult to understand why an HIV positive woman would not choose to abort."[9] And still others found it morally reprehensible that individuals would knowingly and willingly expose others to the risk of a lethal disease.[10] The implication of such statements was to suggest that HIV-positive pregnant women had an "allegedly deficient 'moral universe'" that compromised their ability to be good mothers.[11] These women were sources of contagion not just medically but also morally, and their claims to the contrary made no sense to many.

Attempts to silence or render nonsensical the voices of HIV-positive women were particularly noticeable in the debates surrounding New York State's 1997 "Baby AIDS Bill." The bill, introduced by Assemblywoman Nettie Mayersohn, was designed to mandate that newborns be tested for HIV and their results disclosed to public health officials, thus enabling infected or at-risk infants to receive proper care. Advocates for HIV-positive women filed a class action lawsuit challenging the constitutionality of the bill and calling it an invasion of women's rights to privacy, bodily integrity, medical decision making, and informed consent.[12] They reminded the public that learning the HIV status of a newborn actually revealed the woman's illness rather than the baby's illness and would not, in and of itself, lead to either women or children receiving the care they needed.[13] Supporters of the policy were appalled by such arguments and saw the lawsuit as part of a larger effort to subordinate the medical needs of "helpless children" to the rights of women.[14] From Mayersohn's perspective, for example, opposition to the Baby AIDS Bill and the resulting failure to test and treat newborns was simply "cruel," "irrational," and "criminal." Indeed, she argued that were the bill to fail, those who opposed it and advocated for women's rights would have to take responsibility for neglecting infants and sentencing babies to a premature death, as well as for undermining the moral fabric of society. According to Mayersohn's arguments, it was perhaps women's opposition to mandatory testing that threatened children even more so than their HIV status.[15]

Supporters of mandatory HIV testing did not come right out and say that it was HIV-positive women who were threatening the lives of their children through their "irrational" or "unacceptable" behaviors and decisions. Yet this was the message implicit in framing the controversy over mandatory testing as a conflict or clash between an infant's right to health care and life and a woman's right to privacy. If arguments for women's rights were to hold off the implementation of mandatory testing, infants' chances at life would be severely reduced, and many would, according to Mayersohn, be sentenced to a "premature death." It was thus upto the state "to stand in place" of these infants, to protect them from neglect and abuse. "These babies," she argued, "if they were able to give consent, would be pleading for protection just as adults living with AIDS are insisting on state of the art medical treatment. We in the State Legislature decided to stand in place of the infant."[16] From Mayersohn's perspective, it was the moral and legal duty of the state to institute mandatory testing and to speak on behalf of those who could not speak for themselves.

By framing the debate as one in which infants' rights to life and health care were in jeopardy, supporters of mandatory testing raised the question of who was to blame for the potential violation of rights, of who was responsible for neglecting these infants and denying them access to health care and life. Supporters' arguments suggested that women were responsible for neglecting infants, and that the threat they posed as bad mothers resided not only in their ability to transmit the virus to their newborns but also, and perhaps more important, in their decisions to favor voluntary testing measures. In other words, it was a woman's choice to oppose mandatory testing that marked her as a dangerous individual. Rights claimed on behalf of infants thereby called into being the identification of HIV-positive pregnant women with the bad mother, the deadly vector of contagion.

It was this figuration of women as "bad mothers," and the continued focus on women as vessels and vectors of contagion, that opponents of mandatory testing attacked in and through their rights claims.

The "Rights" Response

Throughout the first decades of the AIDS epidemic, then, HIV-positive and at-risk women of childbearing age were repeatedly separated from the general public in the United States through the speech acts depicting them as bad mothers. Because they posed a threat to the public health and well-being, HIV-positive women were then treated differently from the rest of the population; their rights were restricted, their needs unmet, and their claims deemed incomprehensible—all in an effort to prevent HIV transmission to others.[17] Despite such treatment, a group of HIV-positive women and their advocates made rights claims to challenge such policies. Indeed, they engaged in the kind of persuasive politics I described in chapter three, knowing that their attempts to challenge a particular policy, as well as the meaning and configuration of womanhood, motherhood, and citizenship articulated therein, might be unsuccessful.

While supporters defended mandatory HIV testing as commonsensical and lifesaving public health policy that few "caring" people could oppose, a broad coalition of feminists, AIDS activists, public health experts, ethicists, and legal experts joined forces in the 1990s to challenge the medical and legal basis of such policies.[18] They did this through a series of rights claims that offered alternative understandings of responsible motherhood. Though they agreed about the importance of preventing mother-to-child HIV transmission, they vehemently objected to mandatory testing as the means to reach that end. Mandatory newborn testing, opponents contended, was poorly timed since by the time an infant's HIV status was learned it would be too late to prevent infection in the first place. Moreover, other forms of mandatory testing alone could not reduce MTCT; reduction would require the kind of medical interventions and behavior changes that, unless forcibly mandated by the state, were contingent upon the voluntary participation of women. Such participation would result, opponents argued, only by building trust between women and medical professionals and this very trust would be undermined by placing doctors in a position to police women's reproductive and health decision making. It would only be in protecting women's rights, such as the right to privacy and informed consent, that an effective response to the problem of MTCT, as well as women's own HIV infection, would arise.

At the heart of opponents' claim that women's rights—to privacy, bodily integrity, informed consent, and medical decision making—ought to be acknowledged and protected were some very traditional depictions of the rights-bearing subject. Opponents of mandatory testing represented HIV-positive women as individuals who had the same rights, needs, and interests as others and whose needs would be best served by limiting the power of the state over their lives. They drew on legal cases and the public discourse of individual autonomy and human dignity to make these claims, calling on policymakers to "start with the assumption that women have the same rights to autonomous determinations of life choices as do men"[19] and to treat women "like other adults in the level of autonomy and privacy afforded them in making" decisions regarding HIV testing and treatment.[20] Moreover, opponents of mandatory testing counseled HIV-positive women to recognize themselves as autonomous and rational decision makers. For example, Executive Director Rebecca Denison, of Women Organized to Respond to Life-threatening Disease (WORLD), suggested that a woman "should not feel pressured or forced to accept a treatment she doesn't want." Decisions about testing and treatment should "be up to her" and not lead to her being punished or denied health care.[21] Such claims were echoed by other activists elsewhere. The New Jersey Women and AIDS Network (NJWAN), for example, created a handbook directed at HIV-positive women that explicitly encouraged them to recognize that they "have the RIGHT to be informed and to be a part of all the decisions made about your body. [And] a RIGHT to be treated with respect and to receive good health care, education and counseling."[22]

On first glance, it would appear that opponents of mandatory testing, whether they made claims in the courtroom, through the media, or in other arenas, were invoking rights claims as trumps. They seemed to present women as individuals who were in possession or ownership of certain rights and to frame the problem as one of policymakers simply failing to appreciate this fact about the world. Policymakers, their arguments suggested, would have to change their positions once they were able to recognize that women had certain rights, whether naturally or by virtue of the hand they had been dealt thanks to the particular political society in which they lived. And debate about mandatory testing policy would then come to a clear end.

But women's rights advocates did far more than simply make a constative utterance stating a fact about the world or play a trump card that was simply unfelicitious. Indeed, they did much more than demand that HIV-positive women be included in a group from which they were being excluded and did not simply rely on and reinforce notions of atomistic individualism. Taking a closer look at the different ways that opponents of mandatory testing made rights claims, we can see that women's health advocates simultaneously made visible and called into question the constitution of HIV-positive women as noncitizens. They did this in a number of ways that are obscured when we fail to appreciate the full extent of the performativity of their speech acts. For example, women's rights advocates depicted HIV-positive and at-risk women as victims of an unresponsive health-care system and, in so doing, exposed the contradiction between claiming to care about the health of the public and yet excluding the health needs and concerns of a portion of that public. They also made claims for women's rights that relied on figuring women as good mothers who were already invested in properly caring for their offspring. This, in turn, shed light on the complicated relationship that motherhood has always had to citizenship, and on the ways in which women's status as rights-bearing subjects was so very contingent on their being good mothers. Indeed, implicit in the demand for women's right to make medical decisions for themselves and their children was a question about whether or not mothers were ever really full citizens if certain understandings of improper mothering could disqualify them from rights so easily. And in presenting HIV-positive women as thoughtful adults and concerned patients having to make sense of conflicting demands and medical advice, women's rights advocates reached out not just to the rationality of their interlocutors but to their sentiments and emotions as well. The rights claims made by and on behalf of HIV-positive pregnant women can, thus, be understood as claims of persuasion through which new forms of political subjectivity were enacted.

This was very much the case with HIV-positive women, pregnant or not. In making rights claims on behalf of these women, opponents of mandatory testing revealed a host of contradictions. They challenged supporters' implicit presumption that all women have a natural maternal instinct to care for their children but that HIV-positive women are, for some reason, devoid of that. They made visible the contradiction between treating women as vessels and vectors of contagion while purporting to see them as rights-bearing citizens and individuals with needs of their own, and they challenged the idea that one could effectively protect or improve the public health simply by excluding or constraining a large portion of that population. Moreover, they created community among themselves, in coalition with a wide-range of supporters, and even with those who sought to reject that sense of community.

The story of Rosa, a 27-year-old Dominican plaintiff in a suit against the Baby AIDS Bill, is illustrative of the complexity of such rights claiming. In making rights claims on Rosa's behalf, opponents of the law depicted her in a variety of ways that, according to those who brought suit, were quite representative of HIV-positive women's experiences. Rosa, they explained, was not demanding to be recognized by the state or by others around her as an atomistic individual. She was not arguing that her rights should take precedence over the needs and interests of her child's. She was not asking that she be considered an individual whose social context and social relationships were irrelevant to her status as a rights-bearing subject. To the contrary, Rosa was asking to be recognized as embedded in and encumbered by a series of relationships, and it was the specific nature of her relationality—with her child, her doctor, her community— that necessitated not only that she make rights claims but that they be heard as well.[23]

Rosa had to be understood not as someone who was excluded from the community and the general public but as the victim of an unresponsive health-care system. Like many women in her situation who relied on public health-care services, she did not know that she was HIV-positive when she became pregnant. She only learned of her illness several weeks after the birth of her daughter, when a health-care worker called to report that the results of her daughter's mandatory HIV test were positive. Though Rosa had received prenatal care prior to her delivery, she had not known that her daughter would be tested upon birth, nor that she could have had a prenatal HIV test, nor even that her daughter's test would actually indicate her own HIV status.[24] Knowledge of the test results did, however, lead her to stop breastfeeding when she learned that breast milk was a known, though somewhat uncommon, route of HIV transmission. Furthermore, had Rosa been offered testing prenatally, had she been informed immediately that taking AZT during pregnancy might reduce the likelihood of perinatal transmission, and had she been told that breast-feeding increases the likelihood of perinatal transmission, she would have made different decisions, taken different actions. She would have done what other members of the general population assumed good mothers, those who were part-takers in the community, would do. As Rosa stated in her affidavit, "I would have wanted to increase the chances that my child would not have the virus."[25]

Far from making selfish and irresponsible decisions as supporters of mandatory testing suggest, Rosa's choices and actions had been, to a great extent, determined by a health-care system and a society that has long devalued the decision-making capacities, and thus the participation, of poor women of color. Protecting women's rights to privacy and informed consent, bodily integrity and medical decision making, opponents argued, would actually enable this participation and result in better public health outcomes. Acknowledging Rosa's right to privacy, for example, was not meant to license irresponsible behavior or abstract her from her social context. Rather, it was meant to both empower and protect her. Acknowledging Rosa's right to privacy would mean putting energy into voluntary testing programs and improving health-care services. It would mean encouraging her participation in the health-care decisions that would affect her life and the life of her child, providing her with information and access to services. And it would mean a shift away from the continued stigma and disdain that HIV-positive pregnant women were experiencing, a stigma not associated with other high-risk birth situations.[26]

In making claims for Rosa's rights, opponents of mandatory testing were making claims of persuasion rather than trumping claims.[27] They were presenting Rosa's perspective on the world and asking others to see and understand it, at both an intellectual and an emotional level. Their claims for Rosa's rights did not necessarily celebrate or reify her status as a victim but instead made it visible so as to challenge it. Recognizing that her rights and her health were being violated were simply the first steps in transforming Rosa's status from victim to empowered participant in crucial health-care decisions.[28] As one HIV Law Project employee understood it, their job was not about defending purely self-interested individuals. Quite to the contrary, according to affidavits from the other HIV-positive plaintiffs in the lawsuit, all said that "they would have tested if they had known the importance of prenatal testing and had been offered voluntary testing. All would have taken medication to reduce the chances of passing the virus to their children. None of the women would have breastfed."[29]

In demanding that women of childbearing age be recognized as rights-bearing citizens, opponents of mandatory testing challenged depictions of women, implicit in supporters' arguments, as unfit, irresponsible, and irrational mothers. At the same time, in presenting women simultaneously as mothers and rights-bearing subjects, opponents shifted the images of HIV-positive childbearing women from guilty party to victim and from victim to empowered participant, from uncaring bad mother to nurturing good mother. In the process of making rights claims—a process of envisioning women as rights-bearing subjects in a variety of ways—opponents contested and transformed the longstanding representation of HIV-positive women as bad mothers and worked to have them recognized as socially located and socially constituted subjects.

At times, opponents of mandatory testing invoked another narrative about HIV-positive women in the process of making rights claims. I call this the "conflicted woman" narrative. The conflicted-woman narrative depicted HIV-positive women as guided less by uncomplicated and transparent feelings of maternal responsibility than torn between complicated and less-than-satisfying options. The conflicted woman struggled to make sense of what, in the realm of difficult choices, would make the most sense for both herself and her child at a particular time. She was the woman who failed to be tested or decided to forgo AZT treatments, not because she was a victim of inadequate health care but, rather, because she had her own health to consider. The conflicted woman, as represented in opponents' arguments, expressed complicated feelings about her pregnancy and her role as a mother in an attempt to see herself as both a distinct individual and a mother.[30]

What distinguished the conflicted woman from the good mother or the victim was her expression of conflict, her struggle with the responsibilities of motherhood, and her confusion about her own interests and needs. Rather than subsuming women in their identities as mothers or completely disaggregating their interests from those of their children, the conflict narrative presented HIV-positive women as struggling to understand and act on their identities as both pregnant and HIV-positive individuals. Though invoked less often than the good mother or the victim narratives, the story of the conflicted woman was used to complicate the notion of "bad" mothering behavior, to call into question the idea of a transparent maternal instinct, and, once again, to contest the repeated representation of women as conduits of contagion. Like the more traditional representations of women as autonomous, this story about HIV-positive women functioned to individuate women, rendering their own health-care needs visible rather than obscuring them through an exclusive focus on infant care.

What I am suggesting here, by highlighting the different ways in which opponents articulated HIV-positive women's rights-bearing subjectivity, is that opponents not only made multiple kinds of rights claims but even in claiming a single right, such as the right to privacy, they engaged in a variety of speech activities, all of which should be recognized as part of the performance of political subjectivity. In claiming that HIV-positive women have a right to privacy, opponents referenced, explicitly and implicitly, different norms ranging from norms of liberal individualism to those of proper mothering, and from norms about human dignity to those about the sanctity of the doctor-patient relationship. In so doing, opponents challenged invasive state power as well as the disciplinary power of maternal ideology. They deconstructed the speech acts of supporters in order to reveal race and class biases, contextualized women's lives and mothering, and even reimagined mothering by denaturalizing the idea of an instant and unambivalent maternal-child bond. In making rights claims, opponents of mandatory testing worked to make HIV-positive women visible as agents with voices and needs of their own, as individuals who were struggling with their own, and quite often complicated, notions of good mothering. Opponents thus engaged in many of the strategies of resistance that feminists have suggested are necessary to "break mothering free of ideological encapsulation."[31] This kind of rights claiming, I am suggesting, is a performative practice that both challenges and reconfigures identity and community while at the same time serves as a practice through which political subjectivity comes into being.[32] And it is one that occurs far beyond the borders of the United States, particularly in a country such as South Africa.

HIV and Rights in South Africa

South Africa presents a unique opportunity to consider the relationship between rights and democracy and the performative possibilities of rights claiming in the age of AIDS. The Constitution of the Republic of South Africa, crafted in 1996 as the country transitioned from an apartheid state to a democratic nation, is one of the most progressive constitutions in the world. In addition to granting its citizens political and civil rights, it provides protections against discrimination on the basis of gender, ethnicity, and sexual orientation; guarantees rights to religious, cultural, and linguistic communities; and grants its citizens the right to access health-care services including those services associated with reproductive health care.

Of course, what is written on paper and what is done in practice does not always coincide. This is particularly true for the country's female population living with HIV/AIDS. Not only is South Africa the country hardest hit by the AIDS epidemic on the globe, but there, as in many other African and developing nations, women, often of childbearing age, represent the most vulnerable and fastest growing group of individuals to be infected with HIV.[33] With up to 40 percent of HIV-positive women in South Africa falling between the prime childbearing ages of 25 and 29, estimates suggest that without medical intervention, somewhere between 50,000 and 70,000 infected babies would be born each year. The majority of infants born with HIV/AIDS would and often did go on to live very short and sickly lives that drain the emotional, financial, and public health resources of families, health-care workers, and the country as a whole.

As I mentioned earlier, in 1994, AIDS researchers discovered that they could radically reduce the likelihood of mother-to-child HIV transmission (MTCT) by giving an anti-retroviral drug (ARV) such as AZT, and later Nevirapine, to pregnant women and newborns. In many parts of the world, this news was celebrated as a major breakthrough in AIDS prevention and treatment, and both the World Health Organization (WHO) and the United Nations urged countries to adopt policies to prevent mother-to-child HIV transmission (PMTCT). They even provided guidelines to help policymakers design testing, counseling, treatment, and support programs. In South Africa a conversation began in earnest about how best to control the spread of HIV and address the needs of women and children. Discussions about prevention and treatment, about the costs and burdens of caring for those infected and affected by AIDS, and about the rights of individuals and the responsibilities of states led to plans for a national PMTCT program.

Unfortunately, these plans were dealt a major blow in the late 1990s, when government officials, under the leadership of then President Mbeki, became increasingly skeptical about the efficacy, safety, and costliness of instituting a drug regimen for a predominantly poor, rural population.[34] Swayed by arguments that AIDS drugs were highly toxic, that HIV might not cause AIDS, and that a PMTCT plan would come with an exorbitant price tag, public health officials stonewalled efforts to get AZT to pregnant women throughout the country.[35] Their resistance to the plan was so strong that it was able to withstand the onslaught of scientific evidence illuminating the benefits of AZT and even an offer of free drugs from the manufacturer of Nevirapine.

In 2002, the Treatment Action Campaign (TAC), South Africa's largest civil society organization devoted to AIDS activism, took the South African government to task for its AIDS policy, or lack thereof. They launched both a grassroots and a legal campaign to demand a government-sponsored program that would provide citizens with the medical treatments necessary to prevent HIV transmission from mother to child. At the grassroots, TAC began a campaign to address the stigma associated with HIV/AIDS and to increase medical and scientific literacy among those most directly affected by the disease. On the legal front, TAC sued the Minister of Health, demanding that the rights granted in the South African constitution—the rights of access to health care, to dignity, and to equality—be promoted in the case of HIV-positive pregnant women. TAC's defense of the rights of women and children relied heavily on arguments about protecting children from harm and supporting good mothering practices. This emphasis must be understood in the context of the South African "field of experience," where social policy tends to draw on a fairly traditional discourse of motherhood, itself part of a larger South African discourse on gender that often reinforces women's inequality. Not only are women expected to be the primary caretakers of the home and children, confined to traditional gender roles and often at the physical, emotional, and financial mercy of partners and husbands, but the subordination of women is reinforced by a variety of cultural norms and traditions. For example, customary laws allow for men to have multiple wives and divorce or abandon wives at will. These laws can also be used to deny women rights to property.[36] In addition, South African ideals and norms of masculinity often promote men's sense of sexual entitlement, tacitly accepting that violence against women may be an unfortunate consequence of the male sex drive and by taking a cavalier attitude with regard to rape.[37]

This is not to suggest that traditional conceptions of motherhood constitute the whole discourse of motherhood in South Africa, but it is to underscore that in South Africa, as in many other nations around the world, it remains dominant. It is certainly far more prevalent than other discourses of motherhood, such as the Afrikanner discourse emphasizing white women's ruggedness and practicality rather than their passivity or compassion or the African discourse that values motherhood outside of the context of heterosexual marriage.[38] Such "counter" discourses do exist, but they do not have the same kind of influence over public health policy and leadership as the more traditional discourse. And while it may be the case that a post-apartheid maternalism represents an improvement over earlier discourses of motherhood that explicitly devalued African women's mothering, it does not necessarily advance women's equality to the extent needed. Thus, despite the existence of alternative sets of norms and practices, the dominant discourse of motherhood in South Africa mirrors the dominant discourse in many other parts of the world that reinforce women's inequality and devalue the motherhood of poor and racially stigmatized women.

What TAC did, and continues to do, through the making of rights claims on behalf of HIV-positive women and their children is to work with and against these norms about and conceptions of motherhood, often engaging in what Rosalind Petchesky calls strategies of accommodation and resistance.[39] The organization, that is, engages in a variety of practices that sometimes challenge the dominant discourse of motherhood and some-times use it strategically in other contexts. They try to balance efforts to achieve what would be considered feminist ends by using what at times might be considered maternalist means. One of the best representa-tions of this practice comes from TAC's efforts to make the voices of HIV-positive women heard.

When TAC began, there was a dominant belief that having HIV was at odds with being a good citizen, let alone a good mother. If having HIV was a crime worthy of being stoned to death, transmitting the virus to another being, particularly an "innocent" baby, was something one could not even begin to admit. Though they did not come right out and say this, such a message was implicit in the actions of President Mbeki's and even Presi-dent Zuma's administration for a time. Mbeki refused to make AZT avail-able to public hospitals around the country because he worried about the toxicity of the drug. He argued that it was irresponsible of the government to put women in harm's way.[40] Unfortunately, his concern about women's health did not coincide with an effort to protect them from HIV in the first place. Thus, in doing little to address the rampant spread of HIV/AIDS, political leaders not only failed to combat the stigma associated with the disease but also fueled the belief that HIV infection and motherhood—or, rather, impoverished motherhood—were at odds.

To challenge the stigma associated with AIDS, to promote the equality of HIV-positive individuals, and to engender an overhaul of national AIDS health policy, TAC took to the streets, the airways, and eventually the courtroom with the 2002 case of *Minister of Health v. Treatment Action Campaign*. At the center of their efforts to garner government and public support for PMTCT programs throughout the country were the stories of HIV-positive women themselves, stories of grief and loss, pain and struggle, fear and frustration. These stories called into question the con-ceptions of HIV-positive motherhood implicit in the policymakers' posi-tion while providing HIV-positive women with an outlet to express their emotions and an opportunity to become civil society leaders themselves. HIV-positive women spoke at protests, marches, and rallies, gave inter-views to the media, and provided legal affidavits to the court; and in so doing they offered a different version of HIV-positive motherhood from the one presented by the government. The women portrayed themselves as first and foremost mothers who desperately wanted to do what was in the best interests of their children. While some admitted to feeling shame and guilt for placing their children at risk of infection, they refused to be condemned or ask forgiveness for the actions. They had done nothing wrong to require either; they sought only to be the best mothers they could be.

The story of Sarah Hlalele offers just one of many examples. As an HIV-positive pregnant woman and TAC volunteer, she not only knew about how to prevent MTCT but was able to obtain drugs that could help her prevent transmission. Unfortunately, she went into labor unexpectedly and gave birth to her son in a hospital without any AIDS treatment program. In an affidavit provided to the Constitutional Court, she recounts the tragic impact of the government's decision to deny AVR treatment to women at publicly funded hospitals. Because she had given birth at a hospital near her home and had gone into labor prematurely, she was unable to gain access to Nevirapine. As a result, her child was born with HIV.[41] Though she had done what she could to prevent HIV transmission and to be a good mother to her child, her efforts were thwarted by the government's policy. This did not stop her, however, from working to make the lives of other HIV-positive pregnant women and their children better. In addition to working tirelessly to care for her own children, she became active in helping other women avoid similar fates. At her funeral, she was hailed as "a courageous mother," "who did everything she could to support and care for her children in spite of continuous bouts of illness" only to be thwarted by an irresponsible government.[42]

Nomandla Yako's story reiterates a number of these themes. She gave birth at a hospital that had no PMTCT program and was neither tested at birth nor offered ARVs to prevent transmission. Because she had no knowledge of her HIV status, she did not ask about AIDS drugs. As she explains in an interview, "Had I known, I would have tried by all means to get the treatment to prevent my child from being HIV-positive. It was very painful for me to see all the suffering that he endured. I have so much love for him and try by all means to give him what he needs to make him happy."[43] Like Hlalele, Yako's first concern was her child. If she had had the right information, the necessary support systems, access to ARVs, she would have done whatever was necessary to prevent transmission and be a good mother to her child, and having a right to access health care would have made this possible.

What becomes clear from the way these women frame their stories and make their rights claims is that the culprit in this story is the government not the women. If the government had acted differently, if it had provided PMTCT programs that supported women's desire to be responsible, protective mothers, much heartbreak, pain, and death could have been avoided. Through their stories, these women not only demanded that the blame for the spread of disease be placed squarely with the government and that public health officials rather than HIV-positive individuals be held accountable for any and all failures to protect children from harm but they also re-presented HIV-positive women, the majority of whom are poor and black in South Africa, as good mothers and valuable citizens.

The stories of women who had no idea that they were putting their children at risk of infection, of mothers sitting at the bedside of terribly ill children watching them die, of women frustrated and angry that they could not do what they understood to be their job populated the news media and raised both the public's awareness and its ire. These disturbing stories and images helped to mobilize HIV-positive women, health-care professionals, and many others by making the fight for PMTCT programs "tangible, understandable, emotive, and life saving."[44] And they were ex- tremely effective. The media used the stories of angst-ridden and grief- stricken mothers to charge the government with negligence, political maneuvering, and disastrous public health policymaking; the Constitu- tional Court found the government's action unacceptable; and support grew that put pressure on political leaders to make changes.

In the end, the court decision, in the case of *Minister of Health v. Treat- ment Action Campaign* though a victory for TAC and HIV-positive women, was narrowly tailored and focused on ordering the government to make MTCT treatment and counseling services available to all pregnant women and newborns. The Court had little to say about AIDS prevention and gender discrimination more generally. This suggests that maintaining a focus on the general needs and rights of women while emphasizing the specific issues faced by women as mothers is not easy. Stories of mothers struggling to keep babies from harm are part of the careful framing of the problem that engenders an important policy solution. Moreover, such maternalist emphases successfully mobilized women and the general public. Nonetheless, such stories sometimes obscure the full picture of women's struggle with AIDS in South Africa, with little getting said about how to protect women from infection in the first place. Not surprisingly, then, some women's rights scholars and activists in South Africa have raised concerns about the focus and strategies of AIDS organizations and have called on the feminist community and women's rights organizations to make HIV/AIDS a more important issue on their own agendas.[45]

Such concerns were not and are not lost on those involved with TAC. In fact, TAC has never seen successful litigation or the implementation of

PMTCT programs as their sole goal. The implementation of PMTCT programs has always been part of a larger effort to reshape AIDS care, the public health system, and gender relations in South Africa. As TAC member and lawyer with the AIDS Law Project, Mark Heywood explained,

> Preventing mother to child HIV transmission has benefits that extend far beyond the life saved and grief prevented. An intervention like this could be used by the government to launch a campaign to encourage much more wide-spread voluntary HIV testing, beginning with pregnant women, but soon extending to fathers. It would create an immediate necessity to train more health workers as counselors and to place them at ante-natal wards. It could also be used as a reason to rapidly improve access and quality of primary health care.[46]

TAC's campaign for women's right to access the treatments needed to combat MTCT was always part of a larger effort to articulate and protect a more general right of all citizens to health care. TAC thus reminded the public that HIV-positive women were not simply mothers; they were first and foremost citizens with rights, and the Constitutional Court agreed, to a certain extent. In his opinion, Judge Botha explained that "[a]t issue here is the right given to everyone to have access to public health care services," a right that includes reproductive health care, "and the right of children to be afforded special protection."[47] And these rights were being violated by government's failure to institute PMTCT programs.

TAC's legal and grassroots campaign has not only influenced court decisions but has also had a profound effect on public policy. For example, the 2007–2011 South African National Strategic Plan (NSP) to address the AIDS epidemic makes prevention in general the country's top priority. This requires, the plan acknowledges, what some would consider to be more explicitly feminist goals of empowering women and educating both men and women about women's rights. It also requires the creation of specific programs to alleviate poverty, address gender-based violence, promote HIV testing, and decrease the stigma associated with HIV.

In claiming a right to access health-care services, TAC was, to a certain extent, making a constative claim, stating a fact about what the law says; but they were also making a performative utterance. If we use a theory of performativity to read the rights claiming of TAC, we see the extent to which TAC, and the other organizations and advocates involved in campaigns on behalf of HIV-positive women brought a new political subject into existence. This is particularly true given that they were challenging a traditional discourse that demonized African women's mothering, HIV-positive women's mothering, and black women's status in the community more generally. Moreover, in recent years, the claim for a right of access to health care has grown beyond a focus on access to treatment, beyond concerns with preventing mother-to-child HIV transmission and protecting babies from harm. It now includes claims about the right to know about and have access to various forms of birth control, as well as about having children with HIV-infected partners. In these cases, rights claims to health care become larger claims about a woman's right to sexual pleasure and control over her reproductive decisions and, of course, to her status as a citizen of a democratic nation.

Recall Butler's explanation of the transformative nature of this practice. When we call ourselves names that we are not usually called and, in fact, when we present ourselves as part of a community whose identity is premised on our very exclusion, we make a claim that is both familiar and unfamiliar at the same time. Such claiming is not a simple assimilation of the norm but, rather, a transformation of the norm itself, whether that is a norm about rights-bearing citizenship, proper motherhood, or sexual being. Terms and norms are being invoked and cited in ways that exceed and help shift dominant ways of thinking, being, and doing. What are HIV-positive women doing when they claim a right? If we think about the utterance as an illocutionary act, we can see that the conventions that are being cited in the process of speaking include those embedded in the South African Constitution. In citing the Constitution, HIV-positive women also make visible and challenge notions of community, bringing into being an understanding of the community of which they are members and demanding that the community treat its citizens equally. They are also appealing to the conventions implicit in the liberal political tradition—conventions which suggest that there is value in considering every human being as a discrete individual, that each "I" is a being worthy of being heard and respected.

Conclusion

One could, of course, read the AIDS policy debates in the United States as pitting public health concerns against the protection of women's rights or as the clash between an urgent call for state intervention and a deeply held commitment to individual freedom. And one could read the debates in South Africa as reinforcing a maternal ideology that sets women up as, if not victims of then certainly subordinates to, the state. Indeed, according to a variety of interpretations of the debates, the struggle over the response to MTCT in both the United States and South Africa seemed to bring to light all the dilemmas that suggest rights claiming is a practice at odds with democratic values and practices, whether because it is anti-majoritarian, because it relies on and perpetuates an undesirable kinds of politics and intuitions about human nature, or because it is simply ineffective. But to frame the debates in these ways is to capture only part of what is going on when rights claims are being made. When viewed from the perspective of performativity, we can see that making rights claims is a process through which HIV-positive women, and those who advocate on their behalf, make visible a number of contradictions in the political logic of the day. In the process of the staging of what Rancière calls a politics of dissensus, new forms of political subjectivity become possible. Through the practice of making rights claims, opponents envisioned and created new relationships for HIV-positive women beyond those encompassed in traditional understandings of relations of privacy, and thus engaged in the kind of Foucauldian relational rights politics described in chapter four.

This is not to suggest that opponents were wholly successful in their campaigns to change policy and practice, or to create a political subjectivity that transformed the status quo. In fact, emphasis on the performative nature of rights claiming reminds us to be attentive to the infelicities, paradoxes, and unexpected outcomes of such speech acts. Such outcomes, however, do not mark the failure of rights language but, rather, the unpredictability and uncertainty of any speech activity, or as democratic theorists such as Arendt and Rancière suggest, of any true practice of politics. Recognizing these performative dimensions of rights claiming also shifts our expectations about what the practice can do for us as democratic citizens. While some might find it disturbing to think of rights claiming as a practice of persuasion, the end result of which I may have little capacity to guarantee, I see this as a mark of a hopeful, albeit ever-occurring politics. It makes rights claiming part of a politics of what Foucault would call "permanent provocation."

6

Practicing Democracy

Introduction

"We have rights." "We are human." "SB 1070 violates civil rights." "Being brown is not a crime." These were just some of the messages scrawled on the many signs, banners, and posters carried during protests convened across the nation to challenge Arizona's 2010 immigration law. The S.B. 1070 law, passed in April of 2010, gives police broad powers to detain anyone suspected of being an illegal immigrant and to demand that they show proof that they are in the United States legally. Should a person fail to produce such documentation, he or she can be deported if here illegally, or charged with a misdemeanor if in the country legally. The law, according to legal experts from the American Civil Liberties Union, violates equal protection and First Amendment guarantees such as the right to travel without fear of harassment and the right to freedom of speech.[1] More generally, opponents—whether they are Latino-rights activists, civil rights advocates, sports figures, music stars, or everyday people—consider the bill to be an invitation to racial profiling and a general violation of the rights of those whose skin color is brown or whose primary language is Spanish. They fear that the law will have a detrimental effect on communities, families, and the sense of belonging felt by those who have family members here both legally and illegally. Of course, those who support S.B. 1070 argue that the bill is designed to address a problem that undermines the rights and general well-being of the American public. They defend it as constitutional because it is targeted at those who are doing something that is already illegal, and at the present time, they have the support of a majority of Americans.

Legal opposition to S.B. 1070 may prevent the bill from taking effect and the protests and information campaigns challenging it may change majority opinion in the end. Of course, even if the court battle is successful public opinion could remain unchanged. Whatever the eventual outcome of these debates, it is likely that we will hear commentary and arguments similar to those being offered in response to the California debate about same-sex marriage rights. If the law is overturned, supporters will likely accuse judges of overstepping their bounds to become legislators and of protecting individual rights at the expense of the interests of the people. Opponents could be taken to task for actively undermining the processes of democratic decision making. Supporters might even go so far as to suggest that those who oppose the law on the grounds that it violates certain rights are prioritizing the individual over the community in a way that jeopardizes both the fiscal and the moral health of the United States. Opponents, on the other hand, would be likely to hail the victory as evidence of a commitment to protecting, perhaps even expanding, the rights and freedoms of democratic citizens. And others, though opposed to the Arizona bill and appreciative of a legal decision overturning it, might raise concerns or voice skepticism about the impact of a rights-based challenge to the law. They might remind us that having rights often does little to address the insecurity and injustice that illegal immigrants and their families face on a daily basis. Rights claiming, they could argue, is not the most effective way to address the needs of immigrants, both legal and illegal, for rights are generally impotent when it comes to reimagining and enacting democratic freedom, putting food on the table, or improving working conditions. Victory in the court but problems in practice may strike others differently. Rather than being seen as evidence of the inefficacy of a rights-based challenge, they might view the limits of a rights-based challenge as a reminder that more needs to be done to shore up the philosophical basis and institutional protection of rights. Rights, they may argue, can serve as robust protections against harm and injustice if they are articulated properly, generated through the proper procedures, and backed with adequate and appropriate forms of power. Like those who think rights can and should be some kind of trump card, these commentators might set to work on rethinking or rearticulating the rules of the game of rights claiming.

Of course, there is no guarantee that the rights claims of opponents will be successful. The courts could easily decide that S.B. 1070 is a constitutional law, and such an outcome would generate its own set of questions, concerns, and responses. If this is the case, some will wonder if the broad coalition of individuals and groups formed to protest the law had simply wasted their precious energy and resources. Others might wonder if, regardless of the outcome, the rights campaign will be interpreted as a political event that is inconsistent with advancing democratic self-governance or democratic values. And still others could hail judicial support of the law as evidence of the triumph of democratic decision making. Such varied perspectives on the meaning and implications of rights claiming in Arizona bring me back to where I began: Should individuals and groups committed to democratic practices and values make rights claims to advance their goals?[2]

As I have suggested through this book, answers to this question differ depending on how one understands what it is that rights are and do, as well as how one understands democracy. If we understand both rights and democracy as ongoing, always unfinished projects, rather than as stable objects or specific procedures, respectively, and if we understand rights claiming as a performative practice through which we come to shape and reshape democracy, the answer to the above question would be affirmative. Though rights claiming may not end social and political practices that many find objectionable, though it may not guarantee protection against grievous harm or ensure the desired degree of freedom from external forces, and though it may challenge majoritarian decision making, it is, nonetheless, a practice through which we come to be democratic citizens. Rights claiming, understood as a performative practice of persuasion, provides an opportunity for individuals and groups to form and share ways of seeing the world; to shed light on and reimagine ways of thinking, being, and doing; and to take an active role in the political life of a community.

Reading Rights Claims

To defend rights claiming as a practice through which to cultivate democratic citizenship is to challenge traditional ways of thinking not only about rights but also about democracy. If one understands a rights claim as a statement of fact that should compel assent or an illocutionary utterance that, when made under the appropriate circumstances, should be a felicitous trump card, our focus would be on legal outcomes and our assessment of rights' democratic potential would be quite mixed. The fact is that while the campaign to repeal the British Contagious Diseases Acts was ultimately successful, the fight for women's rights to privacy and control over their own bodies, not to mention equality with regard to matters of sexuality, continues to this day. And while gains have been made on behalf of some gay and lesbian rights in the United States and around the globe, the fact remains that homosexuality is a criminal offense in many countries and gay individuals face the denial of a host of human rights on a daily basis. With regard to women and AIDS, the HIV Law Project's suit challenging New York State's 1997 bill mandating the HIV testing of all newborns was unsuccessful, and despite more than a decade of advocacy on behalf of the rights of HIV-positive and at-risk women, as well as the recommendations of prominent public health experts, many policy-makers in the United States continue to push for mandatory testing of pregnant women and newborns.[3] Even in South Africa, where the legal campaign for women's rights was a success (HIV-positive women and newborns now have the right to receive the treatments necessary to prevent mother-to-child HIV transmission), significant work remains to be done in order to ensure that women and children actually receive this care and that the rights granted in the constitution are protected in the face of the tremendous stigma that continues to attend an AIDS diagnosis.

If one understands democracy as equivalent to majority rule or as the instantiation and stabilization of certain values, then again our assessment of the democratic potential of rights claiming would be rather bleak. We certainly could appreciate that rights claiming extends democratic citizenship, at least in its juridical form, to some previously excluded individuals. And we might even argue that this expansion of rights-bearing subjectivity enables individuals' protection from injury, inequity, or other forms of injustice. But we could not overlook the fact that the history and practice of rights shows that rights claiming is often unable to bring about legal changes desired, and even when it does this, it tends to have little impact on policy and practice. In the cases where rights claiming engenders both legal and social change, such change, scholars remind us, often comes at a significant cost: undermining the fabric of a community, shutting off more creative methods of making change, reinforcing passivity among citizens, increasing state power, and perpetuating forms of capitalist exploitation. On these accounts, rights claiming appears to be a flawed approach to advancing democratic ends and practices, perhaps an activity wholly antithetical to the project of democracy, and the choice seems to be either adopting an alternative approach to oppositional politics or articulating a more robust philosophical ground for our rights claims.[4]

If, however, we shift the way we think about what we are doing when we make rights claims, embracing the idea that rights claiming is a performative practice rather than the means to a particular set of procedures or values we call democracy, then we come to see the relationship between rights and democracy and to understand the democratic character of rights claiming anew. Despite the important philosophical and political insights offered by more traditional assessments of rights claiming, a focus on what happens with respect to the legal or policy implications of rights claiming sheds light on only a small part of what we are doing when we make rights claims. In fact, it unnecessarily reduces rights claiming to a specific kind of speech act. Rights claims, on these accounts, are either constative statements, the truth of which others simply need to recognize, or illocutionary utterances, the felicity conditions of which we simply have not yet correctly identified. Such perspectives do not consider the full dimensions of the speech activity that rights claiming is. If we take seriously rights claiming as a performative practice and emphasize the perlocutionary dimensions of the utterance, much more comes into focus. We come to see that, through the practice of rights claiming, individuals learn to be and shape the meaning of democratic citizenship and community. To put the point differently, rights claiming is a far more complicated speech act than is captured by those understandings that reduce rights claiming to statements of facts or the utterance of hopefully felicitous illocutions. Rights claiming, I have been arguing, is better understood as a practice of engaging in the intersubjective activity of persuasion. But, because it is a perlocutionary speech act, the effects of rights claiming are somewhat beyond the control of the claimant. This makes rights claiming a practice of and an invitation to political judgment.

Making Judgments

Judging, as Linda Zerilli explains, is about giving coherence to the set of facts around us, about making sense of the world in which we live. Often we judge by applying a rule to a given situation, by "subsum[ing] a particular under a universal."[5] Political judgment, however, is a unique kind of sense making or coherence creating. It is more akin, Zerilli argues, to the making of aesthetic judgments than it is to rule application. That is, political judgments, like judgments of taste and pleasure, are about seeing the world differently rather than proving beyond a shadow of a doubt, given the empirical evidence, that something is, say, beautiful or hurtful. All the empirical evidence or the most logical arguments in the world cannot compel another to agree, let alone see, that HIV-positive women or gay men act out of love and a desire to avoid hurting others when they make decisions to have children or get married, respectively. "To judge aesthetically or politically," Zerilli writes, "requires that we count what we know differently, count the flower as beautiful quite apart from its use, count nonheternormative sexual practices as part of the common world, quite apart from whatever social function they might serve."[6] It requires that we display and cultivate a willingness to see the world in new ways, to see it from the perspective of another in ways that alter our sense of what we share.[7] This does not mean that others will necessarily see the world as we do or that we will be persuaded to see it as others do. Nor does it mean that we will always make good judgments about the facts around us. As Michaele Ferguson reminds us, "To say that [we] should make judgments is not to say that we will all from the start be capable of making *good* judgments—judgments that fully acknowledge others and are persuasive to them. . . . Judging is a political skill we learn to do better by practicing it in the company of others."[8] Nonetheless, what is importantly democratic about the kind of judgments that lead us to make and, perhaps, be persuaded by rights claims is that they require us to connect with others and to embrace, or at least accept, the uncertainty of outcomes. Through our efforts to consider what might be persuasive to another, and by calling on our interlocutors to make their own judgments rather than demanding that they accept our view of the world because it is simply "true" or logical, we express a faith in the capacity of others to act, however much this might challenge our desire to control how they act and think.

As I have been suggesting, whether we are making rights claims, finding certain rights claims persuasive, or rejecting the practice itself, we are making political judgments rather than simply stating facts about the world or applying clear rules to specific situations. That we, as rights claimants, may not be able to determine or guarantee the outcome of our rights utterance, despite our clearest intentions or our adherence to citing particular conventions at the appropriate times, is testament to this fact. This does not mean that rights claiming has no discernible effects or that it is a waste of time for those interested in advancing, enriching, and enacting democracy. Quite the contrary. If we understand and analyze rights claiming from the perspective of a theory of performativity, if we recognize rights claiming as an intersubjective practice of persuasion whereby we present the world to an interlocutor as we see it, in ways that draw on reasons as well as emotions and take the interlocutor's perspective into consideration, then we can see rights claiming as a fundamentally democratic activity. It is through the practice of rights claiming that new ways of thinking and being come into existence, that individuals learn and practice being democratic citizens, that political subjectivity is constituted and the boundaries of communities are reconfigured.[9]

Such an argument about what a speaker is doing when he or she makes a rights claim might seem to reinforce the idea that there is a fully present and intentional speaking subject, a doer behind the deed, an "I" who simply uses the tool or instrument of rights to achieve a particular end. The theory of performativity developed in these pages, informed as it is by the writings of Taylor, Arendt, and Butler, among others, suggests something quite different. One makes rights claims as a subject already embedded within a community, a web or network of norms and conventions that, though seemingly obvious, are actually quite illusive. Moreover, one comes to be a subject, in part, through the making of such claims. This was certainly the case for HIV-positive African women in South Africa. Their claims were part of a process of political subjectivization whereby they challenged their status as the unintelligible and took part in the political community despite having been inaudible for so long. In making a claim for a right to treatment, a claim made both to the state and to the general public, HIV-positive women and their advocates at the Treatment Action Campaign did not simply make a claim for women's inclusion, nor did they entrench women in some pre-existing status as the "other." They defamiliarized traditional ideas about HIV and motherhood, as well as about African mothering, and thus claimed a place in the community as citizens with voices or, perhaps more accurately, as citizens-to-be, as individuals who will be counted as citizens in the future. As Linda Zerilli, drawing on Arendt, explains, "a claim to a right is not—or not simply—a demand for recognition of *what* one is; it is a demand for acknowledgement of *who* one is, and more important, of who one might *become*."[10]

The value—indeed, the democratic character of rights claiming—lies not in the end result of winning or legitimating a legal right. As important as such goals may be, it would be a mistake to interpret such a legal artifact as the instantiation of democracy or democratic citizenship. Democratic citizenship comes for the doing—the making of rights claims rather than the having of rights.[11] It is manifest in the activity of persuading rather than in the having been persuasive, in the taking part rather than in already being a part-taker. It is in the process of making claims to others in public, that individuals practice forming opinions and developing perspectives, as well as learn to share these perspectives with others. In both cases, subjects recognize themselves, at least implicitly, as already em-bedded in a community, as shaped by it but also able to shape it. This awareness may come in or be manifest through the process of figuring out what makes a perspective one's own, trying to determine how best to com-municate that perspective to multiple others, or simultaneously citing con-ventions and challenging them. This was certainly what Mill was doing during the campaign to repeal the Contagious Diseases Acts, as well as what AIDS activists were doing in their efforts to challenge the Baby AIDS Bill in New York State. In each case, in making a rights claim, stories were told about the individuals who would be rights-bearing subjects. These stories both called upon and challenged the community's ways of seeing and understanding everything from women's character and sexual re-lationships with men to motherhood and doctor-patient confidentiality. They made visible existing understandings of the relationships between self and other, citizen and noncitizen, rights-bearing individual and the one with no rights, while at the same time challenging these understand-ings by reimagining them in both word and deed.

Moreover, the stories told in the process of making a rights claim took the perspective of interlocutors into account. An HIV-positive women who believes that she should be able to decide how she will deal with her illness and her potential to transmit HIV to a child does not need to explain to herself why that is the case, or at least she does not need to do this over and over again in different ways. But she, or her advocates, do this none-theless in the process of making rights claims. Rights claiming called upon multiple narratives of motherhood and female subjectivity, not all of which were perfectly consistent with each other, reminding us that the claim being made is being made to others who are not a unified group and the claimant is engaged in a form of persuasive speech. These multiple stories reveal, in other words, that the activity of rights claiming is not simply about appealing to reason or applying a specific and single rule to a case. Helpless babies, struggling mothers, determined women—these are the subjects of stories designed to appeal to emotions, to reach inter-locutors through their hearts as well as their heads. Individuals certainly give logical reasons for seeing the world as they do; and I do not mean to suggest that the appeals to emotion are irrational or insincere, but they tap into their own and others' capacities for imagination and creativity in ways that are distinct from the process of rational argumentation.

Returning to the Arizona immigration debate, just as determining the legal effects of making rights claims to contest S.B. 1070 will take time, so too will identifying the performative effects of the activity. Perhaps the rights claims being made in this context will challenge traditional notions of legal residency or citizenship in the United States; perhaps those making claims will recognize themselves as engaged in a process of political subjectivization, at least in retrospect; and perhaps the general understandings of what it means to be Mexican American will shift in and through the process of claiming rights. Illuminating the force of the rights claiming in the context of this immigration debate will require considerably more attention to the specific claims being made and the stories in which these claims are embedded. It will require careful consideration of the conventions cited and transformed, the emotions tapped into, and the relationships identified and reimagined. What a performative analysis of rights claiming can tell us at this point, however, is that we will not understand what is being done when we make rights claims if we start from the premise that rights claiming serves simply to constrain the decisions of democratic majorities, that rights claiming will only be successful if the proper procedures are followed, or that the practice is bound to fail. From the perspective of performativity we can see that making rights claims remains an important part of a robust democracy not because of the results that it engenders but because of the practices into which it draws us.

Notes

CHAPTER 1

1. The term "rights revolution" refers to different sets of ideas and practices having to do with the creation of new individual rights, the increased use of rights language outside the courtroom, and a growing sense of oneself as a rights-bearing subject. See, for example, Epp (1998) and Walker (1998).

2. According to the largest public opinion poll ever conducted, a concern with human rights tops the list of priorities of people around the world. See http://www.gallup-international.com/.

3. On the contemporary dominance of rights language in global politics, see, for example, Beitz (2001), Donnelly (2007), Gutmann (2001), and Ignatieff (2001).

4. On the relationship between "rights" and "claims," see Feinberg (1970).

5. Williams (1991).

6. Waldron (2004), 319.

7. For provocative and competing accounts of the historical origins and development of the idea of rights, whether natural or human, civil or moral, see, for example, An'Naim (1992), Feinberg (1980), Flathman (1976), Hunt (2007), Ishay (2004), Moyn (2010), Tuck (1979), Waldron (1984), and Walker (1998).

8. Rosenberg (1993) sheds light on the fact that success in the courtroom, the winning of a right, may have little impact on actual daily life. He continues to maintain that rights are "much ado about nothing" (2009). For much earlier critiques of the efficacy of rights claiming and their implications for democratic communities, see selections from Bentham, Burke, and Marx in Waldron (1988).

9. I could reference numerous texts here, but for a representative sample, see the following: on the communitarian critique of rights, see Glendon (1991) and Sandel (1996); for a postmodern feminist critique; see Brown (1995, 2000a, 2000b); for a review of the debates in critical legal studies and essays on the paradoxes of rights, see Sarat and Kearns (1997); and for a discussion among critical race

scholars, see Crenshaw et al. (1995). And for key texts in the socio-legal scholarship that inform the arguments of this book, see McCann (1994), Rosenberg (1993), and Scheingold (1974).

10. Few scholars explicitly say that we should give up on rights, but this is often the implication, or at least a feasible interpretation, of some arguments. For a debate about the difference between an outright rejection of rights and a critical reading of them, see the exchange between Baynes (2000) and Brown (2000a) as well as Chambers (2003, 2004) and Zivi (2006). See Bedi (2009) for a recent argument that explicitly rejects rights as the language to use in order to limit government action and determine what constitutes a legitimate decision made by a democratic majority. Though I find Bedi's argument provocative, I do not explicitly engage it in this text because I am working with a more expansive understanding of what a right is and does than Bedi.

11. Among the scholars who take a more optimistic approach to rights or recognize the potential political benefits of revised notion of rights are Arneson (2001), Benhabib (2004), Brettschneider (2007), Cohen (2004), Mayerfeld (2003), Nussbaum (1997), and Sen (2004). Brettschneider offers a compelling account of the compatibility between rights and democracy, one worthy of considerable scholarly engagement. Our work differs in important ways, however, that make such engagement beyond the scope of this book. While Brettschneider's project is to offer philosophical proof that rights-based constraints on majorities are consistent with democratic values, I focus on the way rights claims are used by and productive of democratic citizens. Unlike Brettscheider, who defines democracy as a set of values, I am interested in democracy as a practice. On my account, the democratic potential of rights may reside somewhere quite apart from, and even in light of, the failure of rights claiming to constrain governments or groups of any kind. I would suggest that we are working not only with different conceptions of democracy but also with different conceptions of language. I explore the differences between my approach to rights and some of the other more optimistic arguments in chapter two.

12. Here I am thinking of democratic theorists who take what may be referred to as a radical or an agonistic orientations to politics. See, for example, Honig (1991, 1993), Mouffe (2005), and Rancière (1999, 2010).

13. J. L. Austin (1975) is considered to have inaugurated the particular approach to studying language that has become known as speech act theory, but there are many other important thinkers associated with this body of literature. Moreover, speech act theory encompasses a range of approaches to the study of language, and while it may all share commitment to seeing language as performative, it also contains considerable disagreement and variation with respect to the meaning of performativity, the proper way to study language, and the factors that make utterances work. For a good overview, see Loxley (2007) and Miller (2007). For more traditional understandings of and debates within speech act

theory, see Bach and Harnish (1979), Searle (1970), Searle and Venderveken (1985), and Strawson (1964).

14. For a complementary understanding of the world-making capacities of rights, see Benhabib (2004, 2009). Benhabib builds on the work of Robert Cover to describe human rights norms as "jurisgenerative."

15. Though Flathman (1976) also uses the language of practice to describe his understanding of rights, I find that Ivison's (2008) use of the term is more akin to my own. While both acknowledge that rights claiming is a rule-governed social practice that must be understood in the context of linguistic communities, Ivison emphasizes the fluidity and contingency of these rules to a greater extent than Flathman.

16. Berlin (1999), 149–50.

17. See Marshall (1978). See McClure (1992) for a similar reading of rights in historical context.

18. For a constructivist account of culture adopted by political theorists see, for example, Benhabib (2004) and Song (2007). On the idea of a "cultural politics," see Chambers (2009).

19. As Feinberg explains, "To claim that one has rights is to make an assertion that one has them, and to make it in a manner as to demand or insist that they be recognized" (1970, 251).

20. For example, although the legal code in the United States does not include a right to clean air, one would understand, at least on some level, what a person says when she claims she has such a right. We would recognize that she is suggesting that individuals must have clean air if they are to flourish as human beings and that certain practices—whether governmental, corporate, or social—are so objectionable as to require change, regardless of the economic or political costs. See Feinberg (1992) for other good examples.

21. See Hohfeld (1978) for the classic typology of rights and, for a somewhat revised version of the Hohfeldian typology of rights, see Wenar (2005).

22. On the objective nature of rights, see Strauss (1953), for example, who argues that rights are "natural," as in objective truths that have an ontological or metaphysical status that transcends time and place, and that universally accrue to individuals by virtue of their very nature or humanity. Rights, on this account, reflect moral truths, "standard(s) of right and wrong independent of . . . and higher than" the law and social norms (2). On the socially constructed nature of rights, see, for example, Minow (1987). She argues that rights are legal creations, "the formally announced legal rules that concern relationships among individuals, groups, and the official state" at a particular moment in time (1866).

23. Feinberg (1970). According to Feinberg, claiming is "an elaborate sort of rule-governed *activity*" (250). While I am guided by Feinberg's suggestion to study rules, I find the language of norms and conventions equally useful and, to the extent that I use the language of rules, I also follow Tully (1999) and others who remind us that the rules of any game or any politics are never static.

24. Austin (1975), 6.

25. According to Warnock, performatives can be understood as "a large class of doings . . . which could be said essentially to *consist in* the exploitation or following or invoking of certain conventions . . . saying the words is, counts as, in virtue of the convention, doing the thing" (1973, 71).

26. But even in Massachusetts, the speaker may be doing more than just making a statement. According to Austin, an utterance can be both constative and performative at the same time, for "there is no necessary conflict between (a) our issuing the utterance being the doing of something, (b) our utterance being true or false" (1975, 134). In fact, Austin eventually replaces the constative/performative distinction with the tripartite division associated with what he calls "the theory of speech-acts." According to this theory, an utterance can be examined in terms of its locutionary, illocutionary, and perlocutionary dimensions.

27. Here, then, I depart from the more traditional Skinnerian reading of Austin that emphasizes the intentionality of the speaking subject as the key to the felicity of a claim. See Skinner (2002).

28. Bourdieu (1994), 111.

29. Ibid. Bourdieu continues by saying that "Strictly speaking, there cannot be an illocutionary act unless the means employed are conventional, and so the means of achieving it non-verbally must be conventional. But it is difficult to say where conventions begin and end" (119). For other helpful accounts of the distinction between illocution and perlocution, see Felman (1983) and Kaufman-Osborn (2002).

30. Butler (1997a).

31. Taylor (1985), 232.

32. See Cavell (1976, 1979) and Laugier (2005).

33. Butler (1997a), 14.

34. See Tully (1999) on the relationship between the metaphor of games and the insights of agonistic democracy.

CHAPTER 2

1. Hart (1979). In Haskell's terms, "When I say that I have a *right* to do something—whether it is to exercise dominion over a possession, to enjoy equal employment opportunities, or to express controversial opinions in public—I am not merely saying that I want to do it and hope that others will let me; I am saying that they *ought* to let me, have a *duty* to let me, and will be guilty of an injustice, a transgression against established moral standards, if they fail to do so" (1987, 984).

2. As Austin reminds us, claims can be constative, true or false, and performative at the same time. In fact, it is often the case that a statement of fact is also a perlocutionary act of various kinds (1975, 139). Feinberg makes a similar point

when he notes that even propositional rights claims—claims that seem to simply reflect an existing legal or moral fact—are meant to do something, to have an impact on relationships and the world in which they are articulated: "part of the point of propositional claiming is to *make sure* people listen" (1970, 252).

3. A single speech act actually entails multiple activities, some of which we can map and control, at least partially, others of which we cannot. As I discussed in the previous chapter, recent iterations of speech act theory remind us not only that there are nonconventional aspects of speech acts, perlocutionary effects, which are very much beyond the control of the speaker, but even illocutionary acts have outcomes that are uncertain and unpredictable. While some speech act theorists want to avoid this "failure" through the mapping of felicity conditions, others, such as Derrida (1988) and Butler (1997a), embrace these moments of failure. In fact, neither thinks of a speech act "gone awry" as a failure. Instead, they see these moments as a constitutive aspect of communication itself and a reflection of the fact that we are linguistic beings. From Butler's perspective, these moments of "failure," which she calls excess, are to be exploited and celebrated rather than avoided or contained because they are the moments of political possibility.

4. This is not to suggest that the conception of rights-as-trumps is without its critics or its alternatives but, rather, to note its hegemony or dominance in contemporary politics. On this issue, see, for example, Donnelly (2003), Ignatieff (2001), and Pildes (2000).

5. Dworkin (1978), xi.

6. Waldron (1988), 14.

7. For contemporary popular and scholarly references to the metaphor, see, for example, Donnelly (2003), Frohnen and Grasso (2009), Ignatieff (2001), and Wood (2007).

8. Ignatieff (2001), 21.

9. Nussbaum (1997), 301. For a philosophical discussion of the equivalence between constraints and trumps, see Philip Pettit (1987).

10. Rosenberg's *Hollow Hope* (1993) is well-known for suggesting that winning a right in the courtroom may have little effect on existing policies and practices.

11. On the connections between Ronald Dworkin's work and Lockean liberalism, see Pildes (1998, 2000). For an alternative understanding of Dworkin's work, see Waldron (2000).

12. Glendon (1991), 14. Glendon's work reminds us that rights claims have a performative force that Austin would characterize as perlocutionary. The making of a rights claim, in other words, is not just performative if it achieves a particular policy or legal outcome; it is also performative to the extent that it has an impact on the subjective states of listeners and speakers that have nothing to do with its felicity. Glendon's interpretation of the philosophical underpinnings and political implications of rights claims, however contestable, shifts our attention

from the felicity conditions of the claim to the impact that rights claiming has on how we think of ourselves and our relationship to others as democratic citizens; and, in so doing, it encourages us to consider the extent to which the democratic character of rights claiming is tied up with its perlocutionary force, not simply its illocutionary force. From the perspective of a theory of performativity, Glendon is shedding light on the fact that democratic political practices have importance not just in terms of their procedures, institutions, or effectiveness but also in terms of shaping attitudes and feelings towards the self and other. For examples of Glendon's influence on contemporary debates about rights, see the essays in Frohnen and Grasso (2009).

13. There are compelling arguments to suggest that Glendon may be misinterpreting the philosophical development of the idea of rights, as well as the political implications of contemporary rights claiming. See, for example, Minow (1987) and Petchesky (1995). One could also argue, from the perspective of speech act theory, that Glendon is wrong to suggest that rights talk always and only produces an atomistic individualism. This may be a perlocutionary effect of a rights claim, but like all perlocutionary effects, there is no guarantee that an utterance will produce such a state in the mind of a listener or speaker.

14. Austin (1975), 14–15.

15. According to Strawson, some speech acts work without reference to conventions: "although the circumstances of utterance are always relevant to the determination of the illocutionary force of an utterance, there are many cases in which it is not as conforming to an accepted *convention* of any kind . . . that an illocutionary act is performed" (1964, 443). Strawson's argument throws doubt on the scholarly project of ever identifying the precise reasons that an utterance works.

16. On whether or not rights justifiably constrain democratic majorities, see Bedi (2009) and Brettschneider (2007). One could, of course, trace the debates about the proper relationship between rights and democratic majorities back at least to debates during the founding of the United States.

17. Though many read Ronald Dworkin as depicting the rights-bearing subject as an atomistic individual who uses rights to erect barriers between herself and others, I think this is a misreading of both Dworkin and the liberal tradition. Dworkin explicitly rejects the idea that rights are clear-cut immunities or shields when he argues that rights are not akin to "spectral attributes worn by primitive men like amulets" (1978, 176). They are certainly meant to take precedence over competing considerations of the public good, but that is not in order to shield one individual from another or from society absolutely. Instead, they are meant to be reflections of a society that values fairness and equality, evidence that it shows equal concern and respect for its members. In this respect, rights claiming is an essential part of a democratic society. I would suggest that Dworkin advances something of a "political" conception of rights. Dworkin may posit rights as

antecedent to politics—as a standard by which to judge and limit the actions of a society and government or an instrument that could be brought to bear upon a conflict to provide resolution and closure; nonetheless, he decidedly rejects the idea that rights are natural creations or individual birthrights. Instead, he embraces a constructivist approach in which rights are understood as "independent grounds for judging legislation and custom" based on the "hypothesis that the best political program . . . is one that takes the protection of certain individual choices as fundamental, and not properly subordinated to any goal or duty or combination of these. . . . On the constructivist model, the assumption that rights are in this sense natural is simply one assumption to be made and examined for its power to unite and explain our political convictions" (1978, 177). See also Dworkin (1984). See chapter three of this book, as well as Petchesky (1995) for a provocative rereading of the liberal political tradition.

18. Dworkin (1984), 153.
19. See, for example, the arguments in Burley (2004) and Hunt (1992), as well as Pildes (1998, 2000).
20. For different understandings of what it means to call rights "political" rather than metaphysical or moral constructs, see Beitz (2001) and Ingram (2008).
21. Sen (2004).
22. See Mayerfeld (2003) and Cohen (2004), respectively.
23. Ignatieff (2001), 21.
24. Ibid.
25. Ibid, 56.
26. Sen (2004), 322.
27. Sen (2004), 323.
28. I would suggest we find similar tendencies in the work of Seyla Benhabib. Despite her emphasis on rights claiming as a productive or "jurisgenerative" practice and her embrace of rights claiming as a complicated and often uncertain practice of democratic iteration, the Habermasian dimensions of her argument suggest a commitment to holding certain rules of rights claiming stable at all times.
29. On the valuable effects of rights claiming that exceed legal change, see, for example, Goodale and Merry (2007), Merry (2006) and Silverstein (1996).
30. Rights theorists may not be positing an "authentic, self-consistent, essential subject" as some versions of speech act theory do, but they do emphasize a certain kind of intentionality on the part of the speaking subject and assume linguistic interactions are cooperative. See Pratt (1986) for a critique of the assumptions about the speaking subject implicit in speech act theory.
31. See Derrida (1988) for a discussion of the importance of failure in speech activity.
32. Walzer (2004), 103.
33. Mouffe (2005), 34.

34. Honig (1993), 2.
35. I borrow the idea of an instrumental understanding of politics as depoliticizing, as displacing politics itself, from Honig (1993).

CHAPTER 3

1. To be clear, I am not arguing that critics are wholly wrong to suggest that conceiving of rights as trumps has one or more of these problems but, rather, that these issues are not necessarily attributable to every theory or practice in which a right is conceived of as a trump and, perhaps more important, do not fully account for all that is done in and by making a rights claim.
2. I discuss and challenge these readings of Arendt and Mill at points later in this chapter. For Arendt's critique of rights, see in particular "The Decline of the Nation-State and the End of the Rights of Man" in *On the Origins of Totalitarianism* (1958b). For Mill's defense of rights, see, in particular, *On Liberty* (1991b).
3. Garsten (2006) finds elements of a politics of persuasion in thinkers such as Aristotle and Cicero. On persuasion as a practice central to deliberative democracy, see, for example, Fung (2005).
4. Allen (2004), 61.
5. Arendt (2005b), 15.
6. Ibid., 7.
7. Ibid., 14.
8. Ibid.
9. Arendt (1958a), 184.
10. Arendt (2005a), 129.
11. Arendt (1958a), 222.
12. Arendt (2005a), 93.
13. Arendt (1958b), 292.
14. My interpretation of Arendt's discussion of rights in *On Totalitarianism* differs from those that suggest that her designation of the rights of the citizen as real rights and the rights of man as abstractions means that she was endorsing a nation-state–based understanding of rights whereby the rights of the citizen are the same as the rights of man or rejecting rights all together. See, for example, Rancière (2004). On my reading, an Arendtian understanding of rights as political claims and rights claiming as a practice of persuasion may have more in common with a Rancièrian approach to rights than his work acknowledges.
15. Zerilli (2005), 134.
16. I am not suggesting that rights do not exist in some form or have a particular force. Indeed, they are often legal artifacts that constrain as well as enable us to live in particular ways. My point is that their status as legal artifacts does not tell us all there is to know about the character of rights or the effects of rights claiming.

17. Arendt does not reject truth altogether. She does acknowledge that there are factual truths which encompass information such as which country invades another to start a war. In "Truth and Politics," Arendt distinguishes between rational and factual truths. Rational truths are those that, like mathematical truths, are self-evident and can be discovered in isolation from others. Factual truths consist of information such as when Germany invaded Berlin and which country fired the first shots. Factual truths have a contingent character; they are not self-evident because they could have been otherwise (1968b, 249–51).

Arendt's position, then, is not to discount truth altogether nor encourage "propagandist lying" (Canovan 1974, 113). Rather, Arendt argues that truth, objectivity, and absolute standards should be denied the status of supreme value or absolute necessity (Canovan 1974, 113). Indeed, Arendt wants us to understand that truth threatens political action and human connectedness which are "some of the most essential characteristics of human life" (Arendt 1958b, 297). By foreclosing the possibility of acting in concert and forming connections with others, truth claims and truth seekers produce a life that "is literally dead to the world; it has ceased to be a human life because it is no longer lived among men" (1958a, 176). See also Villa (2000) for a helpful overview of Arendt's thinking.

18. Arendt (2005b), 14.

19. Zerilli (2005), 144.

20. Garsten (2006), 210.

21. For a good discussion of the liberal tradition, its commitment to a particular kind of individual freedom, and the place of Mill's writings within that tradition, see the following: Berlin (1978), DiStefano (1991), Hobhouse (2004), and Ryan (1998).

22. Mill (1991b), 14.

23. See Taylor (1979).

24. Mill (1991b), 15.

25. Mill (1991d), 190.

26. Mill (1991c), 544.

27. Mill (1963b), 837.

28. Ibid.

29. Mill (1952), 191.

30. Mill (1963a), 469.

31. Mill (1963b), 841.

32. Ibid, 839.

33. Mill offers a similar argument in his sharp criticism of Jeremy Bentham. Mill argues that Bentham's theory of human beings as motivated primarily by selfishness and self-interest at all times and in all societies fails to recognize that the "springs" and "motives" of our actions are "innumerable" and diverse, and that human nature is profoundly complex. Only the most vulgar eye, Mill argues, would "assume," as Bentham does, "that mankind are alike in all times and all

places, that they have the same wants and are exposed to the same evils" (1965, 259). Only the poorest analyst of human nature would commit such an intellectual and moral error, obscuring all the diversity and unpredictability of human character.

34. Mill (1963b), 840–41.
35. Mill (1991d).
36. Ibid., 188–89.
37. See Mill (1991a) for a discussion of citizen participation and for a robust defense of Mill as a champion of the democratic practice of deliberation, see Urbinati (2002).
38. This is not to deny that one of the most important social benefits of freedom of expression is, for Mill, the advancement toward "truth." However, I do not want to overemphasize the narrative of progress implicit in Mill's argument. Instead, I want to highlight the fact that Mill values debate and discussion for the effects it has on the character of individuals rather than on the quantity of truth present in a society. For even if society reaches a point where it has replaced all falsehoods with truths, Mill would still defend the importance of freedom of expression.
39. Mill (1991b), 23.
40. Waldron (1987), 414.
41. Mill (1991b), 54.
42. Ibid, 53.
43. Mill (1991d), 152.
44. Mill (1991b), 38–39.
45. Ibid, 59.
46. See Garsten (2006) for a good discussion of the difference between persuasion and manipulation.
47. Mill (1991a), 240.
48. Urbinati (2002), 53.
49. Mill (1991c), 493
50. Garsten (2006), 126.
51. Mill (1963c), 360.
52. Mill (1963c), 1688.
53. Mill (1963c), 356.
54. See Shanley (1998) for a good discussion of the tension in Mill's work that comes from his inability to fully embrace the idea of the artificiality of women's "nature."
55. Mill (1963c), 365.
56. For social histories of the issues raised by the Contagious Diseases Acts, see, for example, Laqueur (1990), McHugh (1980), Spongberg (1997), and Walkowitz (1991).
57. See, for example, Passavant (2002) and Zerilli (1994) for concerns about the implications of Mill's defense of women's rights.

CHAPTER 4

1. In 2000, California voters passed Proposition 22, a measure amending the State Constitution to limit legally recognized marriages to those between members of the opposite sex. This measure was ruled unconstitutional by the State Supreme Court in *In re Marriage Cases*. In 2008, California citizens were given another opportunity to amend their Constitution and they did so by voting in favor of Proposition 8. At the time of this writing, the constitutionality of Proposition 8 is working its way through the court system in the case of *Perry v. Schwarzenegger*.

2. For the State Supreme Court's ruling, see *In re Marriage Cases* 183 P.3d 384 (Cal 2008). The federal district court ruling in *Perry v. Schwarzenegger* is currently being appealed in the Ninth Circuit.

3. On the liberal-communitarian debate see, for example, Taylor (1996), and on deliberative democracy, see Gutmann and Thompson (2004).

4. *Perry v. Schwarzenegger.*

5. Opponents of same-sex marriage counter the charge of discrimination by pointing out that no same-sex couples, whether gay or straight, can get married, and that any opposite-sex couples, again gay or straight, have that right.

6. In interpreting rights claims as utterances that perform various kinds of exemplary citizenship, I am not making a judgment about the value or validity of the arguments on either side of the dispute. While I am persuaded that there is a strong legal and moral case to be made for granting same-sex couples the right to marry, the point of a performative analysis is to highlight the democratic character of the practice, and this entails showing how and why rights claiming provides a language through or a site at which to contest the very meaning and values of democracy.

7. http://www.voterguide.sos.ca.gov/past/2008/general/pdf-guide/vig-nov-2008-principal.pdf.

8. See, for example, the *amicus* brief provided by the Liberty Institute in the case of *Perry v. Schwarzenegger* available at http://www.ca9.uscourts.gov/datastore/general/2010/10/25/amicus3.pdf.

9. This kind of citizenship is expressly enacted through the story of the opposite-sex couple who were high school sweethearts and are now raising gay and straight children. In the California "Voter Information Guide," the parents make an emotional appeal to other similarly responsible, loving, and supportive parents: "All we have ever wanted for our daughter is that she be treated with the same dignity and respect as her brothers . . . . My wife and I never treated our children differently, we never loved them any differently." (http://www.voterguide.sos.ca.gov/past/2008/general/pdf-guide/vig-nov-2008-principal.pdf, 57).

10. As the National Gay and Lesbian Task Force explains in their *amicus* brief, same-sex couples seek "access not only to marriage's state-sponsored benefits but also

to the uniquely valuable social connotations associated with marriage" (filed in *Perry v. Schwarzenegger* and available at http://www.ca9.uscourts.gov/datastore/general/2010/10/27/amicus47.pdf).

11. Ibid.

12. In claiming a right to marriage, same-sex couples and their advocates also make a privacy claim. However, here to, the language shares much in common with the perspectives of those who oppose same-sex marriage rights. The right to marry is defended as a right that limits the size and scope of government power rather than a right that protects a simple interest in doing what one desires. See the California "Voter Information Guide" for the 2008 general election available at http://www.voterguide.sos.ca.gov/past/2008/general/pdf-guide/vig-nov-2008-principal.pdf.

13. Warner (1999), 96.

14. For a rich, contemporary discussion of feminist critiques of marriage, see the symposium "Whatever Happened to Feminist Critiques of Marriage?" in the March 2010 issue of *Politics & Gender* and, in particular, Marso (2010).

15. Warner (1999), 100.

16. Brown (1995), 120.

17. See, for example, Brown (2000a), 470–71.

18. Brown's concerns about rights are not just limited to those made on behalf of particular politicized identities. More recently, Brown (2004) has brought her critique to bear on debates about international human rights by calling into question the ability of human rights discourse and activism to mitigate suffering and respond to injustice. "Human rights activism," she argues, "is a moral-political project," a "particular form of political power carrying a particular image of justice" that actually contributes to the expansion of state power (453). It does this by disenfranchising individuals both psychologically and institutionally, leaving them with "little . . . power to shape collective justice and national aims" (459). Rights claiming neither decreases state power nor empowers citizens. Instead, it functions as a form of power that makes the very goals of rights claiming—to alleviate suffering and enhance human freedom—more difficult. According to Brown, to the extent that making rights claims shapes individuals' sense of self and the contours of political life, it undermines the possibility of alternative visions of justice and forms of political engagement.

19. Brown (1995), 27.

20. Ibid, 28.

21. Ibid, 5. For a compelling response to Brown that addresses the radical democratic potential of rights, see Chambers (2004).

22. To be clear, Brown herself does not suggest that we give up on rights claiming completely. Nonetheless, this is often seen as the implication of such devastating critiques. For a variety of perspectives on these debates see, for example, Brown (2000a), Baynes (2000), Chambers (2004), and Zivi (2006).

23. Foucault (1980), 108. While this may be the source of inspiration for Brown's own efforts to reclaim rights, she never explicitly makes this connection.

24. Foucault (1997a), 162.

25. Importantly, then, Foucault does not use the term "relational rights" in the same manner as some feminists. Relationality, as discussed in recent feminist work, refers to a particular way of understanding the subject of rights as embedded within and influenced by relationships. Relationality is posited as an alternative—indeed, antithesis to atomistic individualism. Foucault's conception of relationality seeks not to establish the "truth" of human nature as relational but, rather, to identify relationships, and the identity categories that are implicated in relationships, as sites of contestation. Indeed, through relational rights, Foucault suggests, marginalized individuals can challenge the norms and disciplinary mechanisms that maintain their subordination. Foucault (1982), 216.

26. While Foucault, himself, is notoriously vague on how it is that making rights claims engenders change and disruption, I think it is fair to consider rights claiming here as a performative speech act, the contestatory potential of which resides in its ability to resignify the very terms deployed. I borrow this understanding from Judith Butler whose discussion of rights as "insurrectionary speech acts" is clearly inspired, at least in part, by Foucauldian notions of agency and resistance (Butler 1997a, 1997b, 2004).

27. Foucault (1997a), 158.

28. Ibid, 160.

29. Foucault also uses the S/M subculture as an example of a relational right for which we might want to struggle. Rejecting the notion that S/M is the reflection or manifestation of natural sexual drives or tendencies toward violence, Foucault argues that "it's the real creation of new possibilities of pleasure, which people had no idea about previously" (1997b, 165). According to Foucault, through practices of S/M, individuals come to relate to each other and to their own bodies in new ways. These practices create a new set of attitudes about pleasure and sexual relationships, as well as new notions of identity and new kinds of behavior absent from more traditional relationships of marriage and family.

30. Foucault (1982), 212.

31. Foucault (1978), 101.

32. Foucault (1982), 221.

33. Theile (1990), 919.

34. Foucault (1982), 222.

35. Butler (2004), 33.

36. Ibid, 32–33.

37. Butler (2000b), 39–40. See also Butler (2000a).

38. Ibid, 39.

39. Butler (2004), 224.

40. Ibid, 30.

41. Ibid, 33.
42. Arendt (1968a), 8. According to Arendt, Lessing believed that humanity was created out of plurality and difference, and was not the result of homogeneity and singularity. He recognized, she explains, that making space for a plurality of voices and perspectives was actually constitutive of friendship and humanity; "he was concerned solely with humanizing the world by incessant and continual discourse about its affairs and the things in it" (30). For without plurality, "the world, which can form only in the interspaces between men in all their variety, would vanish altogether" (31).
43. Here, Arendt reiterates a point made in 1954 in response to an inquiry about her political awakening. Arendt explained that when she finally recognized herself as a Jew, she was compelled to act, and to act as a Jew. Thinking of herself in terms of universals was not helpful, for "if one is attacked as a Jew, one must defend oneself as a Jew. Not as a German, not as a world-citizen, not as an upholder of the Rights of Man, or whatever. But: What can I specifically do as a Jew?" (1994, 12). While it appears that Arendt is rejecting rights in favor of identity here, a careful reading of her criticism of the rights of man in *Origins of Totalitarianism* reveals that she rejects a particular understanding of rights rather than rights per se (1958b). For an interpretation of Arendt's statements about rights to which my own understanding is indebted, see Isaac (1996).
44. Arendt (1968a), 18.
45. Identity for Arendt, as Bonnie Honig (1993) and Lisa Disch (1996) remind us, is performative; it is not what we are, but what we do. Attributes or characteristics such as sex or skin color, even our biological and psychological characteristics, may define *what* we are, but they do not capture *who* we are. "Who" we are, our unique identity, is expressed through our action in the public realm, through our words and deeds (Arendt 1958a, 186).
46. Arendt (1968a), 17.
47. Ibid, 18. I do not mean to suggest that Arendt provides us with a comprehensive theory of identity in this speech. Rather, what I seek to do here is draw out some lessons we might learn from her explicit invocation of Jewishness in the context of an award celebrating the universality of the humanist tradition.
48. Brown (1995) specifically challenges Catharine MacKinnon and Patricia Williams, but similar and more recent arguments about the importance of identity-based rights claims can be seen in the work of Nancy Hirschmann (1999) and Dorothy Roberts (1998).
49. Arendt (1968a), 23.
50. Ibid.
51. Ibid.
52. Ibid, 18.
53. Ibid, 18–19.

54. I am not suggesting that Brown urges us to erase past injustice at all. Rather, I am suggesting that the importance of identity—the bearing it has on future possibilities as well as its resignifiability—is somewhat obscured by Brown's more immediate concern to show the limits of identity-based rights claiming than to suggest their potentialities.

55. Arendt (1958a), 186.

56. Arendt (1968a), 20.

57. This is due, in part, to the fact that our performance of identity is never wholly within our control as actors. "Who" we are is always the indeterminate effect acting and speaking in public, particularly since it comes to be known by the stories told about an individual who acts in the public realm; it is disclosed through the interpretations others make of our political speech and activity (Disch 1996).

58. Butler (2004), 29.

59. Butler (1997b), 104–105.

60. Butler (2004), 33–34.

61. Ibid, 37–38.

62. Butler (1993), 30.

63. Butler (2004), 179.

CHAPTER 5

1. Rancière (1999), 27. For provocative political examples of this practice of placing a wrong in common see, for example, Frank (2010) and Panagia (2006).

2. Quote in Gruson (1987), 8.

3. Prior to the 1994 finding that AZT, when taken by pregnant women and newborns, reduces perinatal transmission from 25% to 8%, little could be done to prevent HIV transmission from mother to child beyond requiring women to forgo or abort pregnancies and avoid breastfeeding. Much of the justification for mandatory HIV testing was built not on clear medical grounds but on a controversial narrative that depicted HIV-positive pregnant women as bad mothers that then stoked a moral panic.

4. See Stoto et al. (1999) for a detailed discussion of the difference between AIDS and other diseases like syphilis or phenylketanuria, for which pregnant women undergo routine tests.

5. See, for example, Corea (1992), and Patton (1993). On concerns about the ethics of mandatory perinatal HIV testing see, for example, Bayer (1990).

6. Quoted in Gross (1987), 1.

7. Quoted in Patton (1994), 107.

8. Quoted in *CDC AIDS Weekly*, October 3, 1988, 2.

9. Quoted in Pies (1995), 329.

10. Kizer Bell (1992). To be fair, Kizer Bell opposed mandatory HIV testing, yet her condemnation of HIV-positive pregnant women echoed those of mandatory testing supporters.

11. Quoted in Ploughman (1995), 187.

12. The HIV Law Project filed a class action lawsuit in 1997 on behalf of a number of low-income women, claiming that the law was unconstitutional and asking the court to order the state to address deficiencies and problems with the existing regulations. The case was unsuccessful. See McGovern (1997) for a review of the arguments. Press releases on file with the author.

13. Opponents argued that because HIV transmission from mother to child can be reduced if the mother receives proper treatment during pregnancy, focus should be on counseling and voluntary testing in the prenatal period. According to some studies, with proper counseling, voluntary testing rates may be as high as 90 percent. Other research suggested that testing acceptance rates varied dramatically and could be as low as 23 percent. The research suggested that a variety of factors, including previous testing, language and cultural barriers, misinformation, and fear of discrimination, influenced a woman's willingness to be tested. For examples of these arguments, see Cooper (1996), McGovern (1997), and Ploughman (1995).

14. Sack (1995).

15. See Zivi (2005) for a more extensive discussion of the ways notions of good and bad mothering informed the debates about mandatory HIV testing of pregnant women.

16. Mayersohn (1997), 727. Etzioni (1999) offers a compelling philosophical defense of mandatory HIV testing of pregnant women and newborns from the perspective of a communitarian critic of rights.

17. This continues in many other countries around the globe, and to a lesser extent even in the United States. Later in this chapter, I discuss the situation as it is manifest in contemporary South Africa.

18. Opponents of mandatory HIV testing of pregnant women and newborns included ACT-UP/New York, the American College of Obstetricians and Gynecologists, the Center for Women's Policy Studies, the Gay Men's Health Crisis, the HIV Law Project, NARAL-NY, and NOW. A more comprehensive list of opponents is on file with the author.

19. Hunter (1992), 30.

20. Hanssens (1996), 1.

21. Denison (1995), 4.

22. Banzhaf (1997), 1. See also Banzhaf, et. al. (1992).

23. This portrait of HIV-positive women as caring, compassionate, and responsible mothers was not an anomaly. Biomedical ethicists, lawyers, and AIDS activists all portrayed HIV-positive women as good mothers to defend women's rights. See Zivi (2005) for a more extensive discussion of these issues.

24. Newborns carry maternal antibodies for up to 18 months after birth. It is the antibodies that reveal the presence or absence of HIV.

25. Quoted in Cynn (1999).

26. According to Rebecca Denison (1995), high-risk HIV pregnancy is treated very differently from high-risk pregnancy of women in their early 40s; "there is no social condemnation of them like what we experience as HIV+ women" (1).

27. I am not suggesting that opponents of mandatory testing necessarily saw themselves as making political claims rather than trumping claims. What I am suggesting is that understanding them as such is more consistent with a theory of linguistic performativity and better allows us to see how rights claiming works.

28. As with Arendt's status as a Jew, the facticity of HIV-positive women's identity is something important to acknowledge before it can be changed. This acknowledgment is not of identity as natural or ontological but as constituted in and through specific relationships at a particular moment in time.

29. Quoted in Cynn (1999).

30. See, for example, Denison (1995).

31. Glenn (1994), 13.

32. As Rancière helps us to understand, political "subjectification" refers to a paradoxical process in which distinctions between self and other, between citizens and noncitizens, are simultaneously acknowledged, challenged, and refigured. Subjectivization redefines "relationships between the ways of *doing*, of *being*, and of *saying* that define the perceptible organization of the community, the relationships between the places where one does one thing and those where one does something else, the capacities associated with this particular *doing* and those required for another. [Political subjectivization] asks if labor or maternity, for example, is a private or a social matter, if this social function is a public function or not, if this public function implies political capacity. A political subject is not a group that 'becomes aware' of itself, finds its voice, imposes its weight on society. It is an operator that connects and disconnects different areas, regions, identities, functions, and capacities existing in the configuration of a given experience." (1999, 40). See also Rancière (1992).

33. Of the more than 30 million individuals living with HIV/AIDS around the globe, 60% are female. The vast majority of people living with HIV/AIDS, 67%, reside in sub-Saharan Africa, 5.5 million in South Africa alone. In both cases, more than half of these populations are women.

34. See Heywood (2003, 2004, 2005) for an extensive discussion of these issues and events.

35. Sidley (2000), 4.

36. See, for example, Heywood & Cornell (1998), 71.

37. Strebel et al., 2006.

38. Walker (1995).

39. Petchesky (1998).

40. Mbeki (1999).
41. Heywood (2003), 309.
42. Mendel (2002).
43. Ibid.
44. Heywood (2009), 20.
45. See, for example, Albertyn (2003, 2005), Albertyn & Meer (2009), Johnson (2006), and Leclerc-Madlala (2008).
46. Heywood (2000).
47. *Minister of Health and Others v. Treatment Action Campaign and Others* (2002).

CHAPTER 6

1. The bill is also being challenged for usurping the federal government's power to regulate immigration.
2. I do not mean to suggest that supporters of a law such as S.B. 1070 do not use rights claims and do not see themselves as committed to advancing democracy. A similar analysis could be done of the campaign to support the Arizona immigration law.
3. In fact, as recently as 2007, New Jersey joined the handful of states that mandate the HIV testing of pregnant women.
4. For an effort to defend rights as reflections of, rather than constraints on, democratic ideals, see Brettschneider (2007).
5. Zerilli (2005), 131.
6. Ibid., 158.
7. Ibid, 162–63.
8. Ferguson (2010), 251.
9. For additional examples of rights claiming as a practice valuable for outcomes apart from legal or policy change, see Correa et al. (2008), Goodale and Merry (2007), Merry (1990, 2006), Petchesky (2003), and Silverstein (1996).
10. Zerilli (2005), 121.
11. For an illuminating example of this, see Zerilli's (2005) reading of the Milan Women's Bookstore Collective.

References

Albertyn, Catherine. 2003. "Contesting Democracy: HIV/AIDS and the Achievement of Gender Equality in South Africa." *Feminist Studies* 29, no. 3: 595–615.

———. 2005. "Defending and Securing Rights Through Law: Feminism, Law and the Courts in South Africa." *Politikon* 32, no. 2: 217–37.

Albertyn, Catherine, and Shamim Meer. 2009. "Citizen or Mothers? The Marginalization of Women's Reproductive Rights in the Struggle for Access to Health Care for HIV-positive Pregnant Women in South Africa." In *Gender, Rights, and Development: A Global Sourcebook*, eds. Maitrayee Mukhopadhyay and Shamim Meer (pp. 27–55). Amsterdam: KIT.

Allen, Danielle. 2004. *Talking to Strangers: Anxieties of Citizenship since Brown v. Board of Education*. Chicago: University of Chicago Press.

An-Na'im, Abdullahi Ahmed, ed. 1992. *Human Rights in Cross-Cultural Perspectives: A Quest for Consensus*. Philadelphia: University of Pennsylvania Press.

Austin, J. L. 1975. *How to Do Things with Words*. Cambridge, Mass.: Harvard University Press.

Arendt, Hannah. 1958a. *The Human Condition*. Chicago: University of Chicago Press.

———. 1958b. *The Origins of Totalitarianism*. New York: World.

———. 1968a. "On Humanity in Dark Times: Thoughts about Lessing." Trans. Clara and Richard Winston. In *Men in Dark Times* (pp. 3–31). New York: Harcourt, Brace, & World.

———. 1968b. "Truth and Politics." In *Between Past and Future* (pp. 227–64). New York: Penguin.

———. 1968c. "What Is Freedom." In *Between Past and Future* (pp. 143–72). New York: Penguin.

———. 1994. "'What Remains? The Language Remains': A Conversation with Gunter Gaus." In *Essays in Understanding: 1930–1954*, ed. Jerome Kohn (pp. 1–23). New York: Harcourt Brace.

————. 2005a. "Introduction into Politics." In *The Promise of Politics*, ed. Jerome Kohn (pp. 93–200). New York: Schocken.

————. 2005b. "Socrates." In *The Promise of Politics*, ed. Jerome Kohn (pp. 1–39). New York: Schocken.

Arneson, Richard. 2001. "Against Rights." *Philosophical Issues* 11: 172–201.

Bach, Kent, and R. M. Harnish. 1979. *Linguistic Communication and Speech Acts.* Cambridge, Mass: MIT Press.

Banzhaf, Marion, ed. 1997. *Pregnancy, HIV, and You: A Handbook for Women with HIV.* New Brunswick: New Jersey Women and AIDS Network.

Banzhaf, Marion, et al. 1992. "Reproductive Rights and AIDS: The Connections." In *Women, AIDS, and Activism*, ed. ACT UP/NY Women & AIDS Book Group (pp.199–210). Boston: South End Press.

Bayer, Ronald. 1990. "Perinatal Transmission of HIV Infection: The Ethics of Prevention." In *AIDS and the Health Care System*, ed. Lawrence Gostin (pp. 62–73). New Haven, Conn: Yale University Press.

Baynes, Kenneth. 2000. "Rights as Critique and the Critique of Rights: Karl Marx, Wendy Brown and the Social Function of Rights." *Political Theory* 28, no. 4: 451–68.

Bedi, Sonu. 2009. *Rejecting Rights.* New York: Cambridge University Press.

Beitz, Charles. 2001. "Human Rights as Common Concern." *The American Political Science Review* 95, no. 2: 269–82.

Benhabib, Seyla. 2004. *The Rights of Others: Aliens, Residents and Citizens.* New York: Cambridge University Press.

————. 2009. "Claiming Rights Across Borders: International Human Rights and Democratic Sovereignty." *American Political Science Review* 103, no. 4: 691–704.

Berlin, Isaiah. 1978. "Two Concepts of Liberty." In *Four Essays on Liberty* (pp. 118–72). New York: Oxford University Press.

————. 1999. "Does Political Theory Still Exist?" In *Concepts and Categories*, ed. Henry Hardy (pp. 143–72). Princeton: Princeton University Press.

Bourdieu, Pierre. 1994. *Language & Symbolic Logic.* Cambridge, Mass.: Harvard University Press.

Brettschneider, Corey. 2007. *Democratic Rights: The Substance of Self-Government.* Princeton: Princeton University Press.

Brown, Wendy. 1995. *States of Injury: Power and Freedom in Late Modernity.* Princeton: Princeton University Press.

————. 2000a. "Revaluing Critique: A Response to Kenneth Baynes." *Political Theory* 28, no. 4 (August): 469–79.

————. 2000b. "Suffering Rights as Paradoxes." *Constellations*, 7, no. 2 (June): 230–41.

————. 2004. "'The Most We Can Hope For . . .': Human Rights and the Politics of Fatalism." *South Atlantic Quarterly* 103, no. 2/3 (Spring/Summer): 451–63.

Burley, Justine, ed. 2004. *Dworkin and His Critics with Replies by Dworkin*. New York: Wiley-Blackwell.

Butler, Judith. 1993. *Bodies That Matter: On the Discursive Limits of Sex*. New York: Routledge.

————. 1997a. *Excitable Speech: A Politics of the Performative*. New York: Routledge.

————. 1997b. *The Psychic Life of Power: Theories in Subjection*. Stanford: Stanford University Press.

————. 2000a. "Competing Universalities." In *Contingency, Hegemony, Universality: Contemporary Dialogues on the Left*, eds. Judith Butler, Ernesto Laclau, and Slavoj Zizek (pp. 136–81). London: Verso.

————. 2000b. "Restaging the Universal: Hegemony and the Limits of Formalism." In *Contingency, Hegemony, Universality: Contemporary Dialogues on the Left*, eds. Judith Butler, Ernesto Laclau, and Slavoj Zizek (pp. 11–43). London: Verso.

————. 2004. *Undoing Gender*. London and New York: Routledge.

Canovan, Margaret. 1974. *The Political Thought of Hannah Arendt*. London: Littlehampton.

Cavell, Stanley. 1976. *Must We Mean What We Say*. Cambridge: Cambridge University Press.

————. 1979. *The Claim of Reason*. Oxford: Clarendon Press.

Chambers, Samuel. 2003. "Ghostly Rights." *Cultural Critique* 54 (Spring): 148–77.

————. 2004. "Giving Up (on) Rights? The Future of Rights and the Project of Radical Democracy." *American Journal of Political Science* 48, no. 2 (April): 185–200.

————. 2009. *The Queer Politics of Television*. New York: Palgrave Macmillian.

Cohen, Joshua. 2004. "Minimalism About Human Rights: The Most We can Hope For?" *Journal of Political Philosophy* 12, no. 2: 190–213.

Cooper, Elizabeth. 1996. "Why Mandatory HIV Testing of Pregnant Women and Newborns Must Fail: A Legal, Historical, and Public Policy Analysis." *Cardozo Women's Law Journal* 3, no. 1: 13–30.

Corea, Gina. 1992. *The Invisible Epidemic: The Story of Women and AIDS*. New York: HarperCollins.

Correa, Sonia, Petchesky, Rosalind, and Richard Parker. 2008. *Sexuality, Health and Human Rights*. New York: Routledge.

Crenshaw, Kimberleé 1995. "Mapping the Margins: Intersectionality, Identity, Politics, and Violence Against Women of Color." In *Critical Race Theory*, eds. Kimberle Crenshaw, Neil Gotanda, Gary Peller, and Kendall Thomas (pp.357–83). New York: New Press.

Crenshaw, Kimberleé, Neil Gotanda, Gary Peller, and Kendall Thomas, eds. 1995. *Critical Race Theory: The Key Writings That Formed the Movement*. New York: New Press.

Cynn, Chris. 1999. "Whose Virus Is It Anyway? Mandatory Testing of Newborns." *Body Positive*, January. http://www.thebody.com/content/art30960.html.

Denison, Rebecca. 1995. "The Hardest Decision I Ever Made." *WORLD Newsletter*, November.

Derrida, Jacques. 1988. "Signature Event Context." In *Limited Inc.* (pp. 1–23). Evanston, Ill.: Northwestern University Press.

Disch, Lisa. 1996. *Hannah Arendt and the Limits of Philosophy*. Ithaca, N.Y.: Cornell University Press.

DiStefano, Christine. 1991. *Configurations of Masculinity: A Feminist Perspective on Modern Political Theory*. Ithaca, N.Y.: Cornell University Press.

Donnelly, Jack. 2003. *Universal Human Rights in Theory & Practice*, 2nd ed. Ithaca, N.Y.: Cornell University Press.

———. 2007. "The Relative Universality of Human Rights." *Human Rights Quarterly* 29, no. 2: 281–306.

Dworkin, Ronald. 1978. *Taking Rights Seriously*. Cambridge, Mass.: Harvard University Press.

———. 1984. "Rights as Trumps." In *Theories of Rights*, ed. Jeremy Waldron (pp. 153–67). New York: Oxford University Press.

Epp, Charles. 1998. *The Rights Revolution: Lawyers, Activists, and Supreme Courts in Comparative Perspective*. Chicago: University of Chicago Press.

Etzioni, Amitai. 1999. *The Limits of Privacy*. New York: Basic Books.

Feinberg, Joel. 1970. "The Nature and Value of Rights." *Journal of Value Inquiry* 4, no. 4: 243–60.

———. 1980. "Duties, Rights, and Claims." In *Rights, Justice, and the Bounds of Liberty: Essays in Social Philosophy* (pp. 130–42). Princeton: Princeton University Press.

———. 1992. "In Defence of Moral Rights." *Oxford Journal of Legal Studies*, 12, no. 2: 149–69.

Felman, Shoshana. 1983. *The Literary Speech Act: Don Juan with J.L. Austin, or Seduction in Two Languages*. Trans. Catherine Porter. Ithaca, N.Y.: Cornell University Press.

Ferguson, Michaele. 2010. "Choice Feminism and the Fear of Politics." *Perspectives on Politics* 8, no. 1: 247–53.

Flathman, Richard. 1976. *The Practice of Rights*. New York: Cambridge University Press.

Foucault, Michel. 1978. *The History of Sexuality: An Introduction: Volume I*. New York: Vintage Books.

———. 1980. [1976]. "Two Lectures." In *Power/Knowledge: Selected Interviews and Other Writings 1972–1977*, ed. Colin Gordon (pp. 78–108). New York: Pantheon.

———. 1982. "The Subject and Power." In *Afterward to Michel Foucault: Beyond Structuralism and Hermeneutics*, by Hubert L. Dreyfus and Paul Rabinow (pp. 208–26). Chicago: University of Chicago Press.

———. 1997a. [1982]. "The Social Triumph of the Sexual Will." In *Ethics: Subjectivity and Truth*, ed. Paul Rabinow (pp. 157–62). New York: New Press.

———. 1997b. [1987]. "Sex, Power, and the Politics of Identity." In *Ethics: Subjectivity and Truth*, ed. Paul Rabinow (pp. 163–73). New York: New Press.

Frank, Jason. 2010. *Constituent Moments: Enacting the People in Postrevolutionary America*. Durham, N.C.: Duke University Press.

Frohnen, Bruce, and Kenneth Grasso, eds. 2009. *Rethinking Rights: Historical, Political, and Philosophical Perspectives*. Columbia, Mo.: University of Missouri Press.

Fung, Archon. 2005. "Deliberation Before the Revolution: Toward an Ethics of Deliberative Democracy in an Unjust World." *Political Theory* 33, no. 2: 397–419.

Garsten, Bryan. 2006. *Saving Persuasion: A Defense of Rhetoric and Judgment*. Cambridge, Mass.: Harvard University Press.

Glendon, Mary Ann. 1991. *Rights Talk: The Impoverishment of Political Discourse*. New York: Free Press.

Glenn, Evelyn Nakano. 1994. "Social Constructions of Mothering: A Thematic Overview." In *Mothering: Ideology, Experience, and Agency*, eds. Evelyn Nakano Glenn, Grace Chang, and Linda Rennie Forcey. New York: Routledge.

Goodale, Mark, and Sally Engle Merry, eds. 2007. *The Practice of Human Rights: Tracking Law Between the Global and the Local*. New York: Cambridge University Press.

Gross, Jane. 1987. "Bleak Lives: Women Carrying AIDS." *New York Times*, August 27, A1.

Gruson, Lindsey. 1987. "AIDS Toll in Children Is Called 'Deadly Crisis,'" *New York Times*, April 9, B8.

Gutmann, Amy. 2001. Introduction to *Human Rights as Politics and Idolatry*. Princeton: Princeton University Press.

Gutmann, Amy, and Dennis Thompson. 2004. *Why Deliberative Democracy?* Princeton: Princeton University Press.

Hanssens, Catherine. 1996. "Mandatory Newborn Testing: A Policy Paper." New York: Lambda Legal Defense and Education Fund.

Hart, H. L. A. 1979. "Between Utility and Rights." *Columbia Law Review* 79: 828–46.

Haskell, Thomas. 1987. "The Curious Persistence of Rights Talk in the 'Age of Interpretation.'" *Journal of American History* 74, no. 3: 984–1012.

Heywood, Mark. 2000. "Confronting AIDS: Human Rights, Law, and Social Transformation." *Health & Human Rights* 5, no. 1: 149–79.

———. 2003. "Preventing Mother to Child HIV Transmission in South Africa: Background, Strategies and Outcomes of the TAC Case against the Minister of Health." *South African Journal on Human Rights* 19, no. 2: 278–315.

———. 2004. "The Price of Denial." *Interfund Development Update* 5, no. 3: 93–122.

———. 2005. "Shaping, Making and Breaking the Law in TAC's Campaign for a National Treatment Plan." *Democratizing Development: The Politics of Socioeconomic Rights in South Africa*, eds. P. Jones and K. Stokke (pp. 181–212). Leiden: Martin Nijhoff.

————. 2009. "South Africa's Treatment Action Campaign: Combining Law and Social Mobilization to Realize the Right to Health." *Journal of Human Rights Practice* 1, no. 1: 14–36.

Heywood, Mark, and Morna Cornell. 1998. "Human Rights and AIDS in South Africa: From Right Margin to Left Margin." *Health and Human Rights* 2, no. 4: 60–82.

Hirschmann, Nancy. 1999. "Difference as an Occasion for Rights: A Feminist Rethinking of Rights, Liberalism, and Difference." *Critical Review of International Social and Political Philosophy: Special Issue on Feminism, Identity, and Difference* 2, no. 1: 27–55.

Hobhouse, L. T. 2004. *Liberalism and Other Writings*. Ed. James Meadowcroft. Cambridge: Cambridge University Press.

Hohfeld, Wesley. 1978. *Fundamental Legal Conceptions as Applied to Judicial Reasoning*. Westport, Conn.: Greenwood.

Honig, Bonnie. 1991. "Declarations of Independence: Arendt and Derrida on the Problem of Founding a Republic." *American Political Science Review* 85, no. 1: 97–113.

————. 1993. *Political Theory and the Displacement of Politics*. Ithaca, N.Y.: Cornell University Press.

Hunt, Alan, ed. 1992. *Reading Dworkin Critically*. New York: St. Martin's Press.

Hunt, Lynn. 2007. *Inventing Human Rights: A History*. New York: W.W. Norton.

Hunter, Nan. 1992. "Complications of Gender: Women and HIV Disease." In *AIDS Agenda: Emerging Issues in Civil Rights*, eds. Nan Hunter and William Rubenstein (pp. 5–40). New York: New Press.

Ignatieff, Michael. 2001. *Human Rights as Politics and Idolatry*, ed. Amy Gutmann. Princeton: Princeton University Press.

Ingram, James. 2008. "What is a 'Right to Have Rights'? Three Images of the Politics of Human Rights." *American Political Science Review* 102, no. 4: 401–16.

Ishay, Micheline. 2004. *The History of Human Rights: From Ancient Times to the Globalization Era*. Berkeley: University of California Press.

Isaac, Jeffrey. 1996. "A New Guarantee on Earth: Hannah Arendt on Human Dignity and the Politics of Human Rights." *American Political Science Review* 90, no. 1: 61–73.

Ivison, Duncan. 2008. *Rights*. Ithaca, N.Y.: McGill-Queens University Press.

Johnson, Krista. 2006. "AIDS and the Politics of Rights in South Africa: A Contested Terrain." *Human Rights Review* 7, no. 2: 115–29.

Kaufman-Osborn, Timothy. 2002. *From Noose to Needle: Capital Punishment and the Late Liberal State*. Ann Arbor: University of Michigan Press.

Kizer Bell, Norah. 1992. "Women and AIDS: Too Little, Too Late?" In *Feminist Perspectives in Medical Ethics*, eds. Helen Holmes and Laura Purdy (pp. 46–62). Bloomington: Indiana University Press.

Laqueur, Thomas. 1990. *Making Sex: Body and Gender from the Greeks to Freud*. Cambridge, Mass.: Harvard University Press.

Laugier, Sandra. 2005. "Rethinking the Ordinary: Austin After Cavell." In *Contending with Cavell* ed. Russell B. Goodman (pp. 82–99). New York: Oxford University Press.

Leclerc-Madlala, Suzanne. 2008. "Global Struggles, Local Contexts: Prospects for a South African AIDS Feminism." In *The Politics of AIDS: Globalization, the State and Civil Society*, eds. M. L. Foller and H. Thorn (pp. 141–55). New York: Palgrave Macmillan.

Loxley, James. 2007. *Performativity*. New York: Routledge.

Marshall, T. H. 1978. *Citizenship and Social Class*. Sterling, Va.: Pluto Press.

Marso, Lori. 2010. "Marriage and Bourgeois Respectability." *Politics & Gender* 6, no. 1: 145–53.

Mayerfeld, Jamie. 2003. "Who Shall Be Judge?: The United States, the International Criminal Court, and the Global Enforcement of Human Rights." *Human Rights Quarterly* 25, no. 1: 93–129.

Mayersohn, Nettie. 1997. "Mandatory Testing of Pregnant Women and Newborns: HIV, Drug Use, and Welfare Policy: The 'Baby AIDS' Bill." *Fordham Urban Law Journal* 24: 721–27.

Mbeki, Thabo. 1999. Address to the National Council of Provinces. Available at http://www.anc.org.za/ancdocs/history/mbeki/1999/tm1028.html, accessed December 16, 2009.

McCann, Michael. 1994. *Rights at Work: Pay Equity Reform and the Politics of Legal Mobilization*. Chicago: University of Chicago Press.

McClure, Kirstie. 1992. "On the Subject of Rights: Pluralism, Plurality, and Political Identity." In *Dimensions of Radical Democracy: Pluralism, Citizenship, Community*, ed. Chantal Mouffe (pp. 108–27). New York: Verso.

McGovern, Theresa. 1997. "Mandatory HIV Testing and Treating of Child-Bearing Women: An Unnatural, Illegal, and Unsound Approach." *Columbia Human Rights Law Review 28*, pp. 469–99.

McHugh, Paul. 1980. *Prostitution and Victorian Social Reform*. New York: St. Martin's Press.

Mendel, Gideon. 2002. "Getting Better." *Guardian*, December 14, pp. 17–36.

Merry, Sally Engle. 1990. *Getting Justice and Getting Even: Legal Consciousness among Working Class Americans*. Chicago: University of Chicago Press.

———. 2006. *Human Rights and Gender Violence: Translating International Law into Local Justice*. Chicago: University of Chicago Press.

Mill, John Stuart. 1952. *Autobiography*. New York: Oxford University Press.

———. 1963a. "An Examination of Sir William Hamilton's Philosophy." In *The Collected Works of John Stuart Mill*, ed. John M. Robson (v. 9). Toronto: University of Toronto Press.

———. 1963b. "A System of Logic." In *The Collected Works of John Stuart Mill*, ed. John M. Robson (v. 7–8). Toronto: University of Toronto Press.

———. 1963c. "The Contagious Diseases Acts." In *The Collected Works of John Stuart Mill*, ed. John M. Robson (v. 21). Toronto: University of Toronto Press.

———. 1965. "Bentham." In *Mill's Essays on Literature & Society*, ed. J. B. Schneewind (pp. 240–89). New York: Collier.

———. 1991a. "Considerations on Representative Government." In *On Liberty and Other Essays*, ed. John Gray (pp. 203–467). New York: Oxford University Press.

———. 1991b. "On Liberty." In *On Liberty and Other Essays*, ed. John Gray (pp. 1–128). New York: Oxford University Press.

———. 1991c. "The Subjection of Women." In *On Liberty and Other Essays*, ed. John Gray (pp. 469–582). New York: Oxford University Press.

———. 1991d. "Utilitarianism." In *On Liberty and Other Essays*, ed. John Gray (pp. 129–201). New York: Oxford University Press.

Miller, J. Hillis. 2007. "Performativity as Performance/Performativity as Speech Act: Derrida's Special Theory of Performativity." *South Atlantic Quarterly* 106, no. 2: 219–35.

Minow, Martha. 1987. "Interpreting Rights: An Essay for Robert Cover." *Yale Law Journal* 96, no. 8: 1860–1915.

Mouffe, Chantal. 2005. *On the Political (Thinking in Action)*. New York: Routledge.

Moyn, Samuel. 2010. *The Last Utopia: Human Rights in History*. Cambridge, Mass.: Belknap Press of Harvard University Press.

Nussbaum, Martha. 1997. "Human Rights Theory: Capabilities and Human Rights." *Fordham Law Review* 66 (November): 273–300.

Panagia, Davide. 2006. *The Poetics of Political Thinking*. Durham, N.C.: Duke University Press.

Passavant, Paul. 2002. *No Escape: Freedom of Speech and the Paradox of Rights*. New York: New York University Press.

Patton, Cindy. 1993. "With Champagne and Roses: Women at Risk From/In AIDS Discourse." In *Women and AIDS: Psychological Perspectives*, Corinne Squire, ed. (pp. 165–87). Newbury Park, Calif.: Sage Publications.

———. 1994. *Last Served? Gendering the HIV Pandemic*. Bristol, Pa.: Taylor & Francis.

Petchesky, Rosalind. 1995. "The Body as Property: A Feminist Re-vision." In *Conceiving the New World Order: The Global Politics of Reproduction*, eds. Faye Ginsburg and Rayna Rapp (pp. 387–406). Berkeley: University of California Press.

———. 1998. Introduction to *Negotiating Reproductive Rights: Women's Perspectives Across Countries and Cultures* by Rosalind Petchesky and Karen Judd (pp. 1–30). New York: Zed Books.

———. 2003. *Global Prescriptions: Gendering Health and Human Rights*. New York: Zed Books.

Pettit, Philip. 1987. "Rights, Constraints, and Trumps." *Analysis* 47, no. 1: 8–14.

Pies, Cherie. 1995. "AIDS, Ethics, Reproductive Rights: No Easy Answers." In *Women Resisting AIDS: Feminist Strategies of Empowerment*, eds. Beth Schneider and Nancy Stoller (pp. 322–34). Philadelphia: Temple University Press.

Pildes, Richard. 1998. "Why Rights are Not Trumps: Social Meanings, Expressive Harms, and Constitutionalism." *Journal of Legal Studies* 27, no. 2: 725–63.

———. 2000. "Dworkin's Two Conceptions of Rights." *Journal of Legal Studies* 29, no. 1: 309–15.

Ploughman, Penelope. 1995. "Public Policy Versus Private Rights; The Medical, Social, Ethical, and Legal Implications of Testing Newborns for HIV." *AIDS & Public Policy Journal* 10, no. 4: 182–204.

Pratt, Mary Louise. 1986. "Ideology and Speech-Act Theory." *Poetics Today*, 7, no. 1: 59–72.

Rancière, Jacques. 1992. "Politics, Identification, and Subjectivization." *October* 61 (Summer): 58–64.

———. 1999. *Dis-Agreement: Politics and Philosophy*. Minneapolis: University of Minnesota Press.

———. 2004. "Who Is the Subject of the Rights of Man." *South Atlantic Quarterly* 103, no. 2/3: 297–310.

———. 2010. *Dissensus: On Politics and Aesthetics*. New York: Continuum.

Roberts, Dorothy. 1997. *Killing the Black Body: Race, Reproduction, and the Meaning of Liberty*. New York: Pantheon Books.

Rosenberg, Gerald. 1993. *The Hollow Hope: Can Courts Bring About Social Change?* Chicago: University of Chicago Press.

———. 2009. "Much Ado About Nothing: The Emptiness of Rights' Claims in the Twenty-first Century United States." *Studies in Law, Politics, and Society* 48: 1–41.

Ryan, Alan. 1998. "Mill in a Liberal Landscape." In *Cambridge Companion to Mill*, ed. John Skorupski (pp. 497–540). Cambridge: Cambridge University Press.

Sack, Kevin. 1995. "House Panel to Draft Bill Requiring AIDS Tests of Newborns." *New York Times*, July 14, A15.

Sandel, Michael. 1996. *Democracy's Discontent: America in Search of a Public Philosophy*. Cambridge, Mass.: Harvard University Press.

Sarat, Austin, and Thomas Kearns, eds. 1997. *Identities, Politics, and Rights*. Ann Arbor: University of Michigan Press.

Scheingold, Stuart. 1974. *The Politics of Rights: Lawyers, Public Policy, and Political Change*. Ann Arbor: University of Michigan Press.

Searle, John. 1970. *Speech Acts: An Essay in the Philosophy of Language*. New York: Cambridge University Press.

Searle, John, and Daniel Vanderveken. 1985. *Foundations of Illocutionary Logic*. New York: Cambridge University Press.

Sen, Amartya. 2004. "Elements of a Theory of Human Rights." *Philosophy & Public Affairs* 32, no. 4: 315–56.

Shanley, Mary. 1998. "The Subjection of Women." In *The Cambridge Companion to Mill*, ed. John Skorupski (pp. 396–422). New York: Cambridge University Press.

Sidley, Pat. 2000. "AZT Tests Not Yet Sufficient, Minister Maintains." *Business Day (South Africa)*, January 12.

Silverstein, Helena. 1996. *Unleashing Rights: Law, Meaning, and the Animal Rights Movement*. Ann Arbor: University of Michigan Press.

Skinner, Quentin. 2002. *Visions of Politics: Volume 1: Regarding Method*. Cambridge, UK: Cambridge University Press.

Song, Sarah. 2007. *Justice, Gender, and the Politics of Multiculturalism*. New York: Cambridge University Press.

Spongberg, Mary. 1997. *Feminizing Venereal Disease: The Body of the Prostitute in Nineteenth Century Medical Discourse*. New York: New York University Press.

Stoto, Michael, Donna Almario, and Marie McCormick, eds. 1999. *Reducing the Odds: Preventing Perinatal Transmission of HIV in the United States*. Washington, D.C.: National Academy Press.

Strawson, P. F. 1964. "Intention and Convention in Speech Acts." *Philosophical Review* 73, no. 4: 439–60.

Strauss, Leo. 1953. *Natural Right and History*. Chicago: The University of Chicago Press.

Strebel, A., M. Crawford, T. Shefer, A. Cloete, N. Henda, M. Kaufman, L. Simbayi, K. Magome, and S. Kalichman. 2006. "Social Construction of Gender Roles, Gender-Based Violence and HIV/AIDS in Two Communities of the Western Cape, South Africa." *Journal of Social Aspects of HIV/AIDS* 3, no. 3: 516–28.

Taylor, Charles. 1979. "Atomism." In *Power, Possessions, and Freedom: Essays in Honour of C. B. Macpherson*, ed. Alkis Kontons (pp. 39–61). Toronto: University of Toronto Press.

———. 1985. "Language and Human Nature." In *Human Agency & Language: Philosophical Papers, Vol. 1* (pp. 215–47). New York: Cambridge University Press.

———. 1986. "Cross-Purposes: The Liberal-Communitarian Debate." In *Liberalism and the Moral Life*, ed. Nancy Rosenblum. Cambridge: Harvard University Press.

Thiele, Leslie Paul. 1990. "The Agony of Politics: The Nietzschean Roots of Foucault's Thought." *American Political Science Review* 84, no. 3 (September): 907–25.

Tuck, Richard. 1979. *Natural Rights Theories: Their Origin and Development*. New York: Cambridge University Press.

Tully, James. 1999. "The Agonic Freedom of Citizens." *Economy & Society* 28, no. 2: 161–82.

Urbinati, Nadia. 2002. *Mill on Democracy: From the Athenian Polis to Representative Government*. Chicago: University of Chicago Press.

Villa, Dana. 2000. "The Development of Hannah Arendt's Political Thought." In *The Cambridge Companion to Hannah Arendt*, ed. Dana Villa (pp. 1–21). New York: Cambridge University Press.

Waldron, Jeremy, ed. 1984. *Theories of Rights*. New York: Oxford University Press.

———. 1987. "Mill and the Value of Moral Distress." *Political Studies* 35, no. 3: 410–23.

———, ed. 1988. *Nonsense upon Stilts: Bentham, Burke and Marx on the Rights of Man*. New York: Methuen.

————. 2000. "Pildes on Dworkin's Theory of Rights." *Journal of Legal Studies* 29, no. 1: 301–307.

————. 2004. "The Rule of Law as a Theater of Debate." In *Dworkin and His Critics*, Justine Burley, ed. Malden, MA: Blackwell Publishing: 319–336.

Walker, Cherryl. 1995. "Conceptualising Motherhood in Twentieth Century South Africa." *Journal of Southern African Studies* 21, no. 3: 417–37.

Walker, Samuel. 1998. *The Rights Revolution: Rights and Community in Modern America*. New York: Oxford University Press.

Walkowitz, Judith. 1991. *Prostitution and Victorian Society: Women, Class, and the State*. New York: Cambridge University Press.

Walzer, Michael. 2004. "Deliberation . . . and What Else?" In *Politics and Passion: Toward a More Egalitarian Liberalism* (pp. 90–109). New Haven, Conn.: Yale University Press.

Warner, Michael. 1999. *The Trouble with Normal*. Cambridge, Mass.: Harvard University Press.

Warnock, G. J. 1973. "Some Types of Performative Utterance." In *Essays on J. L. Austin* (pp. 67–89). Oxford: Clarendon Press.

Wenar, Leif. 2005. "The Nature of Rights." *Philosophy & Public Affairs* 33, no. 3: 223–52.

Williams, Patricia. 1991. *The Alchemy of Race and Rights*. Cambridge, Mass.: Harvard University Press.

Wood, Gordon. 2007. "Natural, Equal, Universal," *New York Times*, April 8.

Zerilli, Linda. 1994. *Signifying Woman: Culture and Chaos in Rousseau, Burke, and Mill*. Ithaca, N.Y.: Cornell University Press.

————. 2005. *Feminism and the Abyss of Freedom*. Chicago: University of Chicago Press.

Zivi, Karen. 2005. "Contesting Motherhood in the Age of AIDS: Maternal Ideology in the Debate over Mandatory HIV Testing." *Feminist Studies* 31, no. 2: 347–74.

————. 2006. "Feminism and the Politics of Rights: A Qualified Defense of Identity-based Rights Claiming." *Politics & Gender* 1, no. 3: 377–97.

Index